Artificial Intelligence and Deep Learning for Decision Makers

A Growth Hacker's Guide to
Cutting Edge Technologies

by

Dr. Jagreet Kaur
Navdeep Singh Gill

FIRST EDITION 2020

Copyright © BPB Publications, India

ISBN: 978-93-89328-684

LIMITS OF LIABILITY AND DISCLAIMER OF WARRANTY

Distributors:

BPB PUBLICATIONS
20, Ansari Road, Darya Ganj
New Delhi-110002
Ph: 23254990/23254991

DECCAN AGENCIES
4-3-329, Bank Street,
Hyderabad-500195
Ph: 24756967/24756400

MICRO MEDIA
Shop No. 5, Mahendra Chambers,
150 DN Rd. Next to Capital Cinema,
V.T. (C.S.T.) Station, MUMBAI-400 001
Ph: 22078296/22078297

BPB BOOK CENTRE
376 Old Lajpat Rai Market,
Delhi-110006
Ph: 23861747

Published by Manish Jain for BPB Publications, 20 Ansari Road, Darya Ganj, New Delhi-110002 and Printed at Repro India Ltd, Mumbai

Dedicated to

Our Parents
Late S. Ajmer Singh and Mrs. Sarbjeet Kaur
S. Balwinder Singh and Mrs. Kulwinder Kaur

Our Children
Dilnawaz Kaur and Haralam Singh
and
Professor Sakattar Singh Sidhu

About the Authors

 **Dr. Jagreet Kaur** is an author and a data scientist. She has been working as a Chief Operating Officer in Xenonstack for the last 5 years. With that, she is also as Chief Data Scientist and Chief Operating Officer in Akira AI. She has more than 14 years' experience in the field of education and research in different areas, such as Database Security, Data Warehousing, Data Science, and Artificial Intelligence. She has done her B.tech from Guru Nanak Dev Engineering College, Ludhiana, and M.tech from Punjab Engineering College, Chandigarh. She completed her Ph.D. with Research Topic "Artificial Intelligence Based Analytical Platform for Predictive Analysis in Health Care".

She started her career as a lecturer in Khalsa College for Women. After that, she worked in different reputed institutes like Guru Nanak Dev Engineering College and Punjab University, Chandigarh, as a lecturer and assistant professor. She also worked as an assistant professor at the Chandigarh College of Engineering and Technology for 6 years.

With 10 years of experience in Artificial Intelligence, Data Science, Academics with Statistical analysis, Practical AI Applications and Decision Science Solutions, she is pursuing her career with Akira Analytics currently, where she is responsible for Planning and Architecting Decision Science and Data Products using Text analytics, NLP, Deep Learning, Machine Learning, and Computer Vision. She is known for understanding, at a deep level, what customers need and want; driving information and analytics strategy; serving a business purpose; and for providing out-of-the-box, legitimate, and robust solutions for problems related to Artificial Intelligence, Data Science, Decision Science, Text analytics, NLP, Deep Learning, Machine Learning, and Computer Vision.

She also possesses an interest in research papers, and she has published 15 research papers, out of which 10 are international and 5 are national. She is also a member of the Reviewer Community in Springer Publisher.

In her leisure time, she likes to attend workshops and conferences and wants to do programming to create different applications.

 **Navdeep Singh Gill** is working as a Chief Executive Officer in Xenonstack and Product Architect in Akira.AI. From the past 8 years, he has been working on Automation, Analytics, and AI for Building AI-first Organizations and Defining Enterprise Data Strategy.

He has more than 15 years' experience in the IT and Telecom industry. During these years, he worked with some of the well-known companies, like Ericsson, Reliance Communications Ltd., and HFCL Infotel.

With over 15 years' experience in Network Transformation, Cloud Infrastructure Solutions, Big Data Solution, Machine Learning, IoT, AI, Digital Transformation, Real-Time Analytics Solutions, IoT Platform, and Analytics and Cloud-Native applications, he is leading the technical and cross-functional teams as well as carrying out deep, hands-on experience through all phases of an engagement, including strategy, conceptual design, proof of concept, and detailed architectural design.

Under his guidance, Xenonstack is building a strong team for Cloud-Native transformation, Enterprise Devops, DevSecOps, Data Engineering, DataOps and MLOPs, and AI Global Managed Services under the umbrella of NexaOps.

He also helps companies to transform to AI-First Organization and Cloud-Native through the strategic application of Data Science and Artificial Intelligence, Platform Strategy and Enterprise Data, and AI Strategy.

About the Reviewer

Dr. Sarbjeet Singh is a Professor in Computer Science and Engineering at the University Institute of Engineering and Technology, Panjab University, Chandigarh. He holds Ph.D. and M.E degrees from Thapar Institute of Engineering and Technology, Patiala, Punjab. He has over more than 15 years of teaching and research experience. He has, to his credit, more than 100 publications in international journals and conferences of repute. His research interests include machine learning, cloud computing, social network analysis, IoT, telecommunication and smart systems. He has successfully completed a research project under the RPS scheme, funded by AICTE, New Delhi in 2012 and currently working on a MeitY, New Delhi sponsored research project dealing with UAV based intelligent monitoring and surveillance systems. He has guided 3 Ph.D. and more than 20 master students for research in different areas of computer science and engineering. Besides this, he has delivered several expert talks in different colleges and universities and is on the panel of BOS of many institutions and universities. Dr. Singh is a Life Member of the Computer Society of India and the Indian Society for Technical Education.

Acknowledgements

First and foremost, we would like to thank God for giving us the courage to write this book. We would also like to thank everyone at BPB Publications for giving us this opportunity to publish our books.

We would like to acknowledge the people who meant a lot to us—our parents, Late S. Ajmer Singh & Mrs. Sarbjeet Kaur, and S. Balwinder Singh & Mrs. Kulwinder Kaur for showing trust in us and giving us the freedom to choose what we desired. We salute you for the selfless love, care, and sacrifice you gave to shape our life. We appreciate our kids—our daughter, Dilnawaz Kaur, and our son, Haralam Singh—for the patience they showed while we wrote our book. Words aren't enough to say how thankful we are to the both of you. We consider ourselves the luckiest to have a lovely and caring family that stands by our side with their love and unlimited support.

We would also like to thank our teachers and our friends for their useful discussions and suggestions, right from deciding topics and writing the concepts to framing the questions.

Lastly, we would like to thank our critics –without their criticism, we would never be able to write this book.

— *Dr. Jagreet Kaur*
— *Navdeep Singh*

Preface

This book is targeted towards business and organization leaders, technology enthusiasts, professionals, and managers who seek the knowledge of Artificial Intelligence and Deep Learning methods. Their aim is to understand what is Artificial Intelligence and what are the Deep Learning methods, which would lead to them understanding how to implement these methods in improving businesses and organizations. This book is organized in such a way that the fundamentals of Artificial Intelligence are firstly emphasized from the basics of human thinking capabilities towards the implementation of machine intelligence for decision-making processes. Then, the design of Deep Learning architecture, in which is a part of Machine Learning techniques, is highlighted within general applications in our current activities. Later in this book, the chapters are divided according to recent case studies, including healthcare, communications, transportation, social interactions, and financial management. Each chapter will feature an elementary explanation of the problems involved in the case study, followed by the design and applications of Artificial Intelligence solutions, analysis of current trends in solving the problems, and outlooks of potential improvements using new technologies. From this book, readers can expect to learn about the concept of Artificial Intelligence and Deep Learning methods and how to use them according to categorized case studies. The readers will be exposed to the applications of the methods, which can help them spark new ideas of solving problems, improve their businesses and organizations, as well as apply the knowledge of the methods in their own fields.

Chapter 1: This chapter describes the introduction of Artificial Intelligence and Deep Learning methods. At first, the concept of the human thinking process, starting from the biochemical responses within the structure of neurons to the problem-solving steps through computational thinking skills, is covered. Then, the thinking concept is adapted to computer architecture, emphasizing the thinking process performed by the computer. This is expanded to a higher level of thinking, namely, intelligence and reasoning capabilities, which is transliterated to the algorithmic approach in the computer programs.

Chapter 2: In this chapter, the use of Artificial Intelligence and Deep Learning methods is used to design and develop models for improving business and organization processes, products, and services. This chapter serves as a bridge between the knowledge exposed in the previous chapters about Artificial Intelligence and Deep Learning methods with the problems in the business and organization.

Chapter 3: This chapter presents the use of Artificial Intelligence and Deep Learning methods for decision making. This includes how the techniques can represent problems in the form of knowledge, which will be utilized to find solutions by using searching strategies. This chapter also addresses several case studies related to decision making (geolocation-based apps like Waze and Google Maps, and customer suggestion features in e-commerce platforms like Lazada).

Chapter 4: In this chapter, the progress of Deep Learning development by Google Inc. is presented. This includes the achievements of intelligent services currently provided by the company and recent exploration by DeepMind, a subsidiary of Google that is working hard on achieving new frontiers in the Deep Learning research. The chapter also discusses the business model of the company towards the use of Deep Learning technologies.

Chapter 5: This chapter discusses the history of cognitive learning by computers and how IBM utilized the use of the capability in building Watson—an intelligent natural language processing service provided to encapsulate the complexity of Artificial Intelligence in developing applications.

Chapter 6: In this chapter, the advancement of the web services, which is incorporated with intelligent capability introduced by Baidu, is presented. The China-leading company in Artificial Intelligence is taking the web services to the next level by introducing Deep Learning in most of its products and services, which can be seen as a potential game-changer for other Silicon Valley giants, including Google and Facebook.

Chapter 7: Social media is the most revolutionized technology ever made in human history. This chapter introduces the role of Facebook in engaging and connecting people by establishing networks of users in the whole world. The chapter also emphasizes the effort of the company that focuses on the research and development, by creating Facebook Artificial Intelligence Research (FAIR), which is responsible for making the networks of users more efficient to be utilized.

Chapter 8: Apple has introduced most of its innovative products and services every year. In this chapter, business strategies employed by the company, especially in adopting Artificial Intelligence and Deep Learning, are presented. The business models and product development with the latest technologies using Deep Learning will be discussed. This chapter tries to elucidate the hints of the next innovations based on the current trends of this highly secretive company.

Chapter 9: Currently, Microsoft has shown interest in joining the race of Artificial Intelligence by redefining the roles of its research department, Microsoft Research. In this chapter, the efforts of the company in contributing to the development of Artificial Intelligence and Deep Learning research is presented. The company's progression in designing its services to prepare the implementation of the technology can be seen in its cloud service, Azure.

Errata

We take immense pride in our work at BPB Publications and follow best practices to ensure the accuracy of our content to provide with an indulging reading experience to our subscribers. Our readers are our mirrors, and we use their inputs to reflect and improve upon human errors if any, occurred during the publishing processes involved. To let us maintain the quality and help us reach out to any readers who might be having difficulties due to any unforeseen errors, please write to us at :

errata@bpbonline.com

Your support, suggestions and feedbacks are highly appreciated by the BPB Publications' Family.

Table of Contents

1. Artificial Intelligence and Deep Learning 1

Structure 1

Objective 1

Artificial intelligence (AI) 2

Importance of AI 2

Capabilities of AI 3

Deep learning (DL) 5

Machine learning versus deep learning 6

Current scenario on machine learning 7

The current scenario in deep learning 8

The exponential explosion of available data 9

The rise of the Graphics Processing Unit (GPU) 10

The invention of advanced algorithms 11

Deep learning and Big Data 11

Introduction to Artificial Neural Networks (ANNs) 13

The single neuron of humans 13

Detailed working for ANN 16

ANN architecture 17

Types of neural networks in AI 18

Neural network architecture types 19

Algorithmic problem-solving approach 22

Preprocessing 23

Dimensionality reduction 23

Scaling 24

Feature selection 24

Model selection 25

Cross-validation 26

Performance metrics 27

Hyperparameter optimization 27

Evaluation of model and predicting patterns 27

Collection of data 28

Preprocessing of data 29

Preparation of data 30

Training of data 30

Steps of implementation 31

Testing of model 32

Conclusion 33

Questions 33

2. **Data Science for Business Analysis** 35

Structure 35

Objective 36

What is data science? 36

Challenges faced by businesses 37

Uncertainty 37

Globalization 38

Innovation 39

Government policy and regulation 39

Diversity 39

Complexity 39

Technology 40

Supply chains 40

Strategic thinking and problem solving 41

Information overload 41

Problems that occur during model development 41

Design and development of models 42

Problems faced by IT organizations while
developing models 44

Artificial intelligence and deep learning
methods to develop models 46

Artificial intelligence (AI) 47

Deep learning (DL) 48

Why DL matters? 48

Usage of deep learning 49

Improvements in the business...49
DL to optimize manufacturing *50*
Time series analysis for business forecasting *50*
DL in bot recommendation...*51*
Predictive and preventive maintenance for industrial IoT *52*
Deep learning in security...*53*
Deep learning in healthcare..*54*
Fraud detection with deep learning neural network.................*54*
Benefits of data science in business analysis.........................55
Conclusion...55
Questions...56

3. Decision Making...**57**
Structure 57
Objective..58
Representation of problems...58
Design and development knowledge representation...........63
Types of knowledge..*65*
Representation..*66*
Knowledge engineering..*68*
Representation techniques...68
Knowledge representation using predicate logic.....................*69*
Knowledge representation using semantic net.........................*70*
Knowledge representation using frames *71*
Knowledge representation using scripts *72*
Knowledge representation issues 72
Mathematical formulations of representing knowledge...........*73*
Model representation..*74*
Analyze real-world problem...*75*
*Strategies for searching possible solutions
from the problem spaces*...*76*
Solution strategy..*77*
Designing Uber maps...*80*

Uber service architecture *81*

Conclusion.. 82

Questions... 82

4. Intelligent Computing Strategies by Google 83

Structure 83

Objective.. 83

The strategies of Google in deep learning exploration......... 84

Research environment by DeepMind
and other services provided to the users................................ 88

AlphaGo *89*

Autonomous cars... *92*

Working of autonomous car.. *93*

Google Play *94*

DeepMind Health Stream application *95*

AI navigation without a map *95*

Deep Q-Network (DQN) *96*

Working of DQN *97*

Business models currently adopted by Google 99

Google business model canvas 100

How Google will impact current businesses? *105*

Google AutoML *105*

DeepLab-v3+.. *106*

DeepMind *108*

WaveNet 108

Tensor Processing Unit (TPU) *109*

Conclusion.. 110

Questions.. 110

5. Cognitive Learning Services in IBM Watson 111

Structure 111

Objective.. 111

The cognitive learning in NLP 112

Cognitive computing... *112*

Features required for a cognitive system 113

Evolution of cognitive system 114

Characteristics of cognitive computing 115

*Difference between artificial intelligence
and cognitive computing* 116

The scope of cognitive computing and systems 117

Use of cognitive computing in NLP 118

Applications of cognitive computing 119

Issues in cognitive aspects of language modeling 121

Cognitive computing landscape 122

IBM Watson 122

Watson solutions 123

IBM Watson Explorer 123

Working with Watson Explorer 128

Improving services with IBM Watson 130

Government 130

Law enforcement 131

Financial services 132

Banking 132

Insurance 133

Healthcare 134

Retail 135

Customer domain 135

Product domain 136

How to impact businesses with IBM Watson 136

Watson Explorer for manufacturing 137

Watson Explorer for customer service and call-center 137

Watson Explorer for retail and e-commerce 138

Watson Explorer for insurance 138

Conclusion 139

Questions 139

6. Advancement of Web Services by Baidu **141**

Structure 141

Objective 141

Baidu web services and its business orientation 142

Market share of Baidu 143

Tools for Baidu 144

Difference between Baidu and Google 147

Business model of Baidu 148

Product strategy 151

Get the best ranking in the Baidu Search Engine 152

Research and technology 153

SWOT analysis 156

Deep learning in Baidu web services 158

Key assets of Baidu 160

Uses of Baidu 163

Major problems of Baidu 164

Uncertain quality of search results 164

Problems in Baidu mobile promotion 164

Next steps of Baidu intelligent web services 167

Conclusion 168

Questions 168

7. Improved Social Business by Facebook 169

Introduction 169

Structure 169

Objective 170

Introduction to Facebook 172

Effects of Facebook on third-party business 174

Benefits of social media in businesses 176

Lead generation 176

Brand exposure and awareness 177

Targeted traffic 178

Market insights – research and competitor monitoring 179

Customer interaction – customer service and feedback 179

Cost-effective marketing techniques 180

Public relations and human resources 180

The current progress of FAIR for advancing socialmedia.. 181

Application of AI in the field at Facebook scale 184

Social media analytics.. 185

Potential use of DL in improving customers
among social media users 188

Conclusion... 195

Questions... 196

8. **Personalized Intelligent Computing by Apple**.....................**197**

Structure 197

Objective 197

Introduction to Apple 198

Apple's marketing strategy *198*

Siri technology.. *201*

AI in Apple: From Siri to the image processing................... 201

Apple uses DNN for face detection *203*

How face ID detection system works 203

True depth camera system... 204

Neural networks.. 204

Anti-spoofing mechanism in Face ID recognition...................... 204

Other benefits of AI on smartphones 205

Innovation on intelligent product development 206

Emergence of Apple products year by year 207

Conclusion... 208

Questions... 208

9. **Cloud Computing Intelligence by Microsoft**........................**209**

Introduction 209

Structure 209

Objective 210

Microsoft Approach to AI 211

Microsoft AI platform - Overview 211

Technical Stack of Microsoft AI platform.................................. *212*

AI services... 212

Cognitive services 213

Azure machine learning... 214

Bot framework.. 214

AI infrastructure 216

Azure ML Studio 217

Azure ML Workbench... 218

Visual Studio (VS) Code Tools for AI... 218

Azure Notebooks 218

Deep learning framework.. 218

Incorporation of DL capabilities in cloud computing..........219

Microsoft business model 222

Microsoft business segments..225

Conclusion..228

Questions..228

CHAPTER 1
Artificial Intelligence and Deep Learning

This chapter introduces you to artificial intelligence and deep learning methods. The concept of the human thinking process starts from the biochemical responses within the structure of neurons and move forward to the problem-solving steps using computational thinking skills. Then, the thinking concept is adapted to computer architecture emphasizing the thinking process performed by the computer. This is expanded to a higher level of thinking, namely intelligence and reasoning capabilities, which is transliterated to an algorithmic approach in the computer programs.

Structure

- Artificial intelligence (AI)
- Deep learning
- Algorithmic problem-solving approach

Objective

By the end of this chapter, we will understand the basic concept of human thinking processes, which is adapted in computational thinking for solving problems.

Artificial intelligence (AI)

Artificial intelligence (AI) is a digital attempt to achieve human level intelligence using different computations of machines. It is a set of advanced technologies that allow machines to sense, understand, act, and learn from humans.

AI is no longer just an ultramodern notion; it's here right now—such as software that senses what we need, recommendation systems that recommend in real-time, and bots that respond to changes in their environment. In this century, companies are already using AI to innovate and grow fast.

Nowadays, AI and deep learning are the latest technologies that are doing much more. They are supporting humans in complex and creative problem-solving by analyzing vast amounts of data and identifying trends that were previously impossible to detect.

For more than 250 years, technological innovations have driven economic growth.

Among earlier innovations, the most critical ones are general-purpose technologies like steam engines, electricity, and internal combustion engines used in cars, trucks, airplanes, and even lawnmowers.

As technology moved fast, we now have more power in our hands than we had in our homes in the 1990s. The essential general-purpose technology of the current era is Artificial intelligence, particularly **machine learning (ML)** and **deep learning (DL)**, that is, the ability of a machine to keep improving its performance without the intervention of humans. In the past few years, ML and DL have become more efficient and widely available. We are now able to build such systems that learn how to perform tasks on their own.

Importance of AI

There are two reasons why AI is important, which are as follows:

- Firstly, we humans know much more than we can express. Also, it is indescribable how we precisely compute things, right from recognizing a small object like a needle to predicting the changes that will occur in the future. Before AI, we couldn't automate many tasks.

- Secondly, AI systems are often tremendous learners. They can achieve staggering performance in a wide range of activities including fraud detection, recommendation systems, retail analytics, computer vision, cybersecurity, and medical diagnosis. Brilliant digital learners are being deployed across the economy and their impact is going to be very intensive.

Similar to other technologies, AI has generated a lot of unrealistic capabilities. In the area of business, it has a significant impact on the extent of earlier general-purpose technologies. Although it is already in use in many companies around the world, the most fruitful opportunities have not yet been mined.

Artificial Neural Networks (ANNs) are complex models that can be used for a different type of computation inspired by the human brain. Nowadays, ANNs are used in many fields including voice recognition, image recognition, robotics, etc. resulting in much advancement in these fields. The significant effects of AI will be extended in the coming decade, as manufacturing, retail, transportation, entertainment, finance, healthcare, law, education, advertising, insurance, and virtually every other industry transform their core processes and business models to take advantage of DL.

Capabilities of AI

Today's AI is super impressive; AI can perform various tasks that can never be possible without machine learning and deep learning. The goal of AI is to create an expert system, for example, systems that show intelligent behavior, learn, demonstrate, explain, and advise its users. Moreover, AI is meant to implement human intelligence in machines so that machines can understand, think, learn, and behave like humans. Today's AI has been able to achieve success in many areas like robotics, computer vision, and natural language processing, expert system, games, and speech recognition. Here are some examples of machines that can be successfully made using the technology of AI:

- **Chatterbot:** A chatterbot is a computer program that conducts a conversation via auditory or textual methods. Such programs are designed to engage in small talk to pass the Turing Test by fooling the conversational partner into thinking that the program is a human. Some chatterbots use sophisticated natural language processing systems, but many scan for keywords in the input and reply according to the matched keywords or the most similar wording pattern from a textual database.

- **Robotics:** Robots learn new things themselves by observing their surroundings, so they learn more things from humans and use them in a better way. It involves mechanical (usually computer-controlled devices) to perform tasks that require extreme precision or tasks that are tedious or hazardous for humans. Also, they can learn from their mistakes, and they can adapt to new environments.

- **Healthcare:** AI plays a significant role in the field of healthcare. AI-based Healthcare systems can help doctors predict the onset of a disease in a patient by comparing the medical data of the patient with historical data. Such machines can also prescribe the most appropriate medication and laboratory tests for the patient.

- **Gaming:** AI plays a vital role in games such as chess, poker, tic-tac-toe, and others, where the machine can think of the considerable number of possible turns based on heuristic evaluation.

- **Vision systems:** These systems understand, interpret, and grasp visual input on the computer. A restaurant takes photographs that are used to figure out the particular type of food on the plates. Physicians use a clinical expert system to diagnose diseases by analyzing the MRI/Scans images. Police use software that can recognize the face of criminals with a portrait made by a forensic artist.

- **Speech recognition:** AI-based intelligent systems are capable of hearing and understanding the language in terms of sentences and their meanings. It can handle different accents, slang words, noise in the background, change in human sound due to cold, and much more.

- **Handwriting recognition:** AI-based handwriting recognition software can read the text written on paper by a pen or on-screen by a stylus. It can recognize the shapes of the letters and convert them into editable text.

- **Banking:** AI helps in the banking industry with chatbots, **anti-money laundering (AML)** tools, pattern detection, recommendation engines, fraud detection, and algorithmic trading.

So far we've discussed what is AI, its importance, and its capabilities. Now let's look at the different subparts of AI starting with deep learning.

Deep learning (DL)

Deep learning (DL) is a subset of ML and ML is a subset of AI, as shown in the following image. If we say, a car is an artificially intelligent system, then we can say that the fuel used in the car is machine learning:

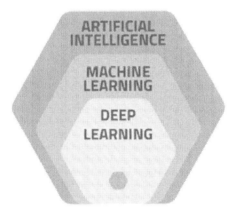

Figure 1.1: Representation of the relationship between AI, ML, and DL

DL is based on neural networks, a conceptual model of the brain. The word *deep* comes from DL algorithms that are trained/run on deep neural networks. The central concept of deep learning is the automatic extraction of representation from data. As our data often appears in the form of discrete information which needs to be joined together for it to make sense, DL and ML use this information and extract features from it to build a broad architecture. This deep architecture explains the data from lower to higher-level functions. It works in a hierarchical order. Data comes from many sources like

Twitter, patient MRI/scans, social media, and sensor data in various forms:

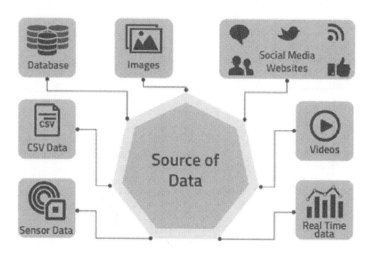

Figure 1.2: *Different sources of data*

Data from these data sources generate 500+ terabytes every day. Thus, there is a need for new ways that can analyze the data. To do this, modern conceptual architecture is required that can work with the massive amounts of data. In other words, it is necessary to recognize how organizations function when they are working with these large datasets. This is where DL comes from. DL algorithms are used to build a model that can extract the data from these data sources and manage it for future predictions, as well as for various other purposes.

When data gets complex, we need to look for an architecture that can handle this kind of data. With time data is turning vast and unstructured, thus an architecture is required that can manage this data correctly. DL solves all these problems. It focuses onworking with complex environments.

Machine learning versus deep learning

Machine learning (ML) is a subset of artificial intelligence. DL is the subset of ML. Let us dive deep into machine learning and deep learning so that we can have a better comparison of them.

Current scenario on machine learning

ML uses various algorithms to parse data, learn from it, and then make a determination or prediction of the problem identified. So, rather than doing hand-coding with a specific set of instructions to accomplish a particular task, the machine is trained using large amounts of data and algorithms that give it the ability to learn how to perform the task.

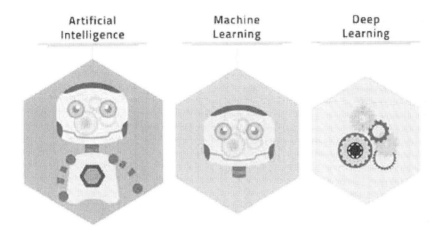

Figure 1.3: *Pictorial representation of AI, ML, and DL*

First of all, the machine needs to train with a vast amount of data. There are several machine learning algorithms that can do this such as the Bayesian Network, Decision Tree, and Clustering. Generally, there are three types of machine learning: supervised, unsupervised, and semi-supervised learning.

Supervised ML is used when a labeled set of features is provided. For example, if the value of x is known, then on the basis of it predict the amount of y. Unsupervised ML differs from supervised ML. In unsupervised ML, you only have to input data x and no corresponding output variables. The goal of unsupervised learning is to model the structure of the data to learn more about the data. Semi-supervised learning fits in between supervised and unsupervised learning. Semi-supervised knowledge is used where there is a large amount of input data x and only some of the data is labeled y. An example of semi-supervised learning is when some of the images are labeled (for example, dog, cat, and person), however, the majority are unlabeled.

Machine learning uses cross-validation to select the complexity of the model. In other words, ML finds the complexity using a small part of the data, and then it tests the model on other parts of the data. Let's explore the different types of learning and their different subtypes in the next figure:

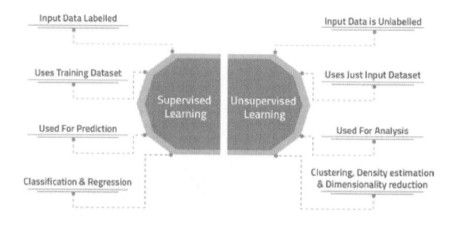

Figure 1.4: Supervised and unsupervised learning with major steps

The current scenario in deep learning

Deep learning is everywhere. It is used to determine which online advertisements to display in real-time; to identify and tag pictures of humans, food as well as animals in photos; to translate voice to text, translate text into different languages; and drive autonomous vehicles.

Deep learning is found in various places. Credit card companies use deep learning models for fraud detection in banks and also to detect whether a credit card can be provided to a particular person or not based on their historical records. Banks use transaction details of customers to detect anomalies in the financial behavior of customers and check whether loans or other facilities should be approved. Hospitals and doctors use it for detection, diagnosis, and treatment of diseases using real-time as well as historical data.

The range of applications is limitless. Other options include text analysis, image analysis, image captioning, image classification, X-ray analysis, stock market analysis, weather forecasting, object detection, finance predictions, and many more.

Deep learning is already used to improve performance, automate processes, detect patterns, and solve problems. DL is continuously improving the performance of machines with automation, pattern recognition in complex structures like proteins and gene expression, and so on.

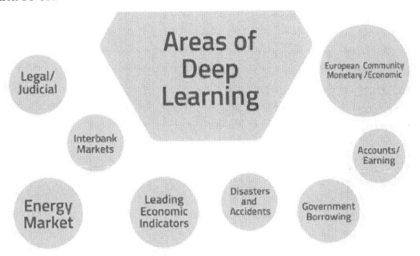

Figure 1.5: Different areas of DL

The following three factors have leveled up the potential for deep learning.

The exponential explosion of available data

A few years ago, there was a time when it was just impossible to analyze petabytes of data. The emergence of Hadoop made it possible to run analytical queries on a vast amount of historical data. We know that Big Data is a buzzword from the last few years, and modern data pipelines are always receiving data at a high ingestion rate. So this constant flow of data at high velocity is termed as Fast Data. Fast data is not just about the volume of data like data warehouses in which information is measured in GigaBytes, TeraBytes, or PetaBytes. Instead, along with measuring the amount of data it also considers the speed of data such as MB per second, GB per hour, and TB per day. So, Volume and Velocity both are considered while talking about Fast Data.

Nowadays, many organizations are trying to collect loads of data regarding their products, services, or their organizational activities such as tracking employee behavior using various methods like log tracking and taking screenshots at regular intervals. Data engineering allows us to convert this data into basic formats, and data analysts turn it into useful results that can help companies to improve customer experience, as well as support them in monitoring and boosting the productivity of employees.

But for cases like fraud detection, log analytics, or real-time analytics, this is not the way to process the data. Imagine, there is a data warehouse like MongoDB which has petabytes of data stored in it. To do the analytics for all the above tasks there is a need to analyze historical data and predict the future.

For such cases, we first need to analyze historical data and predict the faults. It not only requires pre-processing, but it also requires a number of sequential steps that would be taken into account to make effective business decisions for the organization in real-time. It is applicable in anomaly detection, phishing, intelligence, surveillance systems, and many other areas.

Traditionally, high ingestion rate data streaming is managed by storing and processing it; later, this data is taken for further analysis to predict the results and give impacting inferences. But organizations are looking for platforms where they can look into business insights in real-time and act upon them in real-time.

The rise of the Graphics Processing Unit (GPU)

During the '90s, application performance and database throughput were directly proportional to the number of CPUs and available RAM. As these factors are essential to achieving the desired performance of enterprise applications, a new processor was introduced, for example, **Graphics Processing Unit (GPU).**

With the rise of deep learning, GPU now powers many intelligent use cases like autonomous cars, tumor diagnosis, computer vision, recommender systems, speech recognition, etc. Deep learning works on mathematical and statistical computations. **Artificial Neural Networks (ANNs), Convolutional Neural Networks (CNNs),** and **Recurrent Neural Networks (RNNs)** are the modern implementations of deep learning. Every type of neural network such as classification, clustering, and prediction is used with use cases. For example, **Natural Language Processing (NLP)** uses RNNs, while image recognition and face recognition use CNNs.

For instance, a simple image consists of a large matrix of numbers. During the training phase of deep learning, the matrices of these numbers are used as input to the neural network. By training the neural network with thousands of images of a face of a person, the model can quickly recognize a person in a picture. This training process is a correlation of multiple pixels (numbers) to find patterns of faces. The relationship works by multiplying billions of matrices with each other to generate the right result. To increase the training speed, all these operations need to be done in parallel.

CPUs are designed to handle calculations in a sequential order, which means each operation has to perform at its priority and also has to wait for the previous activities to complete. So, to implement the processes in parallel, there is a need to build a processing system that can run processes in parallel. Hence, graphical processing systems were introduced that can handle many operations at a time and perform parallel computation in much less time.

The invention of advanced algorithms

The applications of deep learning in the modern world are vast. Various application fields include speech recognition, learning based on historical data, face recognition, autonomous cars, medical sciences, stock predictions, insurance, and many others.

With the invention of advanced algorithms and computer vision concepts, it became effortless to make a real-time model that helps in facial recognition and speech recognition. Also, deep learning is used to improve NLP tools to understand the meaning of a complete sentence and not just individual words, for example, summarization of text, and identifying sentiments of the person through tweets.

Deep learning and Big Data

In the time of the **Internet of Things (IoTs)** and mobility, with a massive volume of data becoming available at a fast velocity, there must be a need for an efficient analytics system. Also, the variety of data is coming from different types of sources in different formats such as sensors, logs, and structured data from an RDBMS.

In the past years, the generation of data has increased as more applications are being built, and they are generating more data at a faster rate.

Earlier, storage of data was costly, and there was an absence of technology which could efficiently process the data. Now, the storage costs have become cheaper, and the availability of technology to transform Big Data has become real.

Technology-oriented companies such as Google, Yahoo, Microsoft, and Amazon have collected and maintained data that is measured in Exabyte. Also, social media companies such as Facebook, YouTube, and Twitter have millions of users who continuously generate large amounts of data. So, there is a need to analyze this data and produce meaningful results according to the business requirements that can be helpful for decision making.

In addition to analyzing the vast amount of data, there are other challenges such as collection and framing of data, handling unlabeled data, noisy and poor quality data, unsupervised, and uncategorized data. So, here the concept of DL algorithms plays a significant role. These algorithms can automate the system to ingest a massive amount of unlabeled data and automatically extract complex representations.

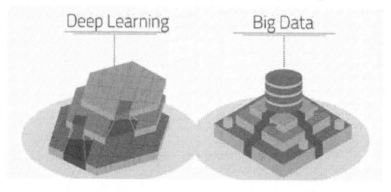

Figure 1.6: Architecture representation of deep learning and Big Data

Deep learning algorithms are architectures of consecutive layers. Each layer works hierarchically, for example, pixels in an image are fed to the first layer, and the output of each layer is provided as input to its next segment.

For instance, in a face detection model, by providing some images of faces as input to the DL algorithm, at the first layer the model can train itself by learning the edges in different orientations. In the second layer, the model uses these edges to learn about more complex features like different parts of a face such as lips, nose, and eyes. In the third layer, the model uses these features to learn even more complex features like different shapes of faces. In the end, the final representations can be used as useful information in applications of face recognition.

Introduction to Artificial Neural Networks (ANNs)

Artificial Neural Network (ANN), computational models based on the essential working of the human brain, changed the whole game of pursuing technology. With the emergence of ANN, now tasks like voice recognition, robotics, and image recognition do not seem to be out of reach. The most significant advantage of ANN is the capability of mapping biological methods in technical ways. It can be understood as a sizeable interconnected web of artificial neurons that can perform specific tasks. These tasks can be specific such as classification, clustering, and pattern recognition.

The single neuron of humans

In a neural network, the basic unit which performs any computation is a neuron. It receives input from other neurons or some external source and computes an output accordingly. Each information has weight (w) associated with it, which is assigned by its relative value to other data. The node applies a function f to the weighted sum of its inputs.

The output from the neuron can be defined as:

Output (O) = f(w1.X1 + w2.X2+b1)

Where *b1* is a bias and *f* is non-linear function and is described as the Activation Function.

The primary purpose of the activation function is to introduce non-linearity into the output of a neuron. Bias is used to provide every node with a trainable consistent value. The typical nerve cell of the human brain is as shown in the following diagram:

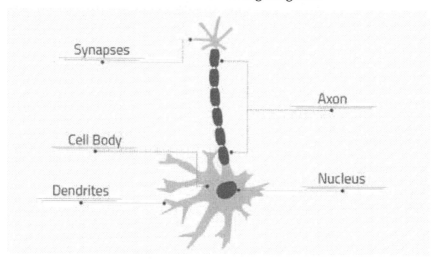

Figure 1.7: Human neuron and its different parts

A human neuron consists of four parts:

- **Synapses:** It can be considered as an internal connection between two neurons. In simple words, you can define it as the quantity of signal transmitted, which is calculated using the weights of the connections.

- **Axon:** It can be understood as the firing mechanism of the signal. When the sum calculated surpasses a specific threshold, the neuron fires the signal, which then travels down to the other neurons.

- **Soma (cell body):** It aggregates all the incoming signals to produce the input.

- **Dendrite:** It performs the task of receiving signals from other neurons.

The following table presents some of the significant differences between ANN and BNN:

Characteristics	ANN	BNN
Speed	Faster in processing information. Response time is in nanoseconds.	Slower in processing information. The response time is in milliseconds.
Processing	Serial processing	Massively parallel processing
Size and Complexity	Less size & complexity. It does not perform complex pattern recognition tasks.	Highly sophisticated and dense network of interconnected neurons containing neurons of the order of 1011 to 1015 of interconnections.
Storage	Information storage is replaceable means new data can be added by deleting an old one	Information storage is adaptable means new information is added by adjusting the interconnection strengths without destroying old information
Control Mechanism	There is a control unit for controlling computing activities	No specific control mechanism external to the computing task.

Figure 1.8: Comparison of the characteristics of ANN and BNN

There are two main similarities between neural networks and the human brain:

- Similar to the human brain, neural networks also gain knowledge using learning.
- The connection strengths are used to store the knowledge of the neuron network, and these are known as synaptic weights.

The comparative similarities between BNN and ANN are as follows:

- In ANN, the weighted inputs based on synaptic interconnection can be considered as equivalent to dendrites in the BNN.
- The neuron unit of ANN can be compared to the cell body of BNN, which is composed of summation and threshold unit.
- In the case of ANN, the output unit can be compared to Axon of BNN.

From the above facts, it is clear that ANN is modeled using the principles of BNN:

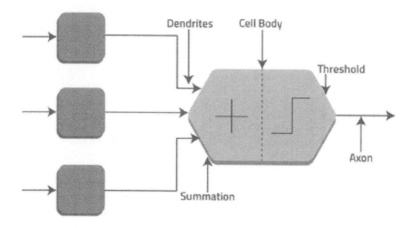

Figure 1.9: Artificial neuron with its different parts

Detailed working for ANN

ANNs are weighted directed graphs that consist of nodes, which are artificial neurons. The connection is established between neuron inputs and neuron outputs using directed edges with which weights are also attached. Let's have an overview of the weighted ANN graph and its layers:

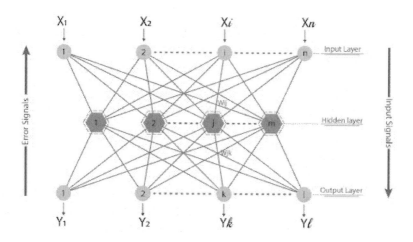

Figure 1.10: Weighted graph of ANN with neurons and its layers.

ANN has the following computational subparts:

- **Weights:** Weights can be understood as the information or knowledge which can be used by the neural networks to provide a solution to a specific problem. Technically, these are the strength of the interconnection between neurons which are situated inside a neural network. The corresponding weights are multiplied with each input respectively

- **Bias:** Bias consists of the information and weights, which is always taken as 1. Technically, inside the computing unit, all weighted data are aggregated. If there is a case when the weighted sum is zero, the bias is used to make the output non-zero by some addition of constant value or for scaling up the system response.

- **Activation Function:** This function is used to get the required output. The output sum from the above is passed through function, and to put up a limit at the arrival of the desired value a threshold value is set up. There are many types of activation, such as linear functions (which is further divided into binary and sigmoid) and nonlinear functions (for example, hyperbolic sigmoidal functions). Some of the activation functions are explained here:

  o **Sigmoidal hyperbolic:** This function has an S-shaped curve. Here the hyperbolic function is used to approximate output from net input. The function is defined as - $f(x) = (1/(1+ e(-\sigma x)))$ where σ - *steepness parameter.*

  o **Binary:** The output has only two values, for example, 0 and 1. For this, the threshold value is set. If the net weighted input is greater than 1, the output is assumed 1 otherwise 0.

ANN architecture

In the architecture of ANN, the neural network consists of many smaller units known as artificial neurons which are arranged in the following series of layers:

- **Output layer:** The prime function of this layer is to respond to the information according to the learning of a particular task. These responses come from the units described above.

- **Input layer:** The function of this layer is to import input as data into the network. On this data, the system starts learning, recognizing, and performing different types of processes.

- **Hidden layer:** This layer lies between the input and the output layers. The function of this layer is to change the information into a format that can be used by the output progressively.

In most of the neural networks, the input layer is fully connected to the hidden layer, and the hidden layer is fully connected to the output layer:

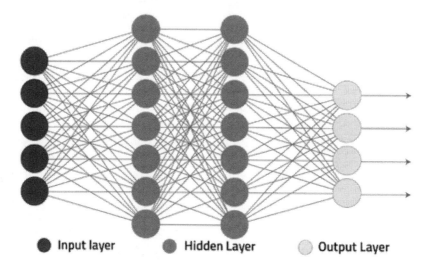

Figure 1.11: Representation of the different layers of ANN

Types of neural networks in AI

There are several types of ANN. Based on the human brain neurons and network functions, an ANN executes tasks similarly. The different types of ANNs are as follows:

Parameter	Types	Description
Based on connection pattern	FeedForward, Recurrent	**FeedForward:** These graphs have no loops. **Recurrent:** Loops occur because of feedback.

Based on the number of hidden layer	single layer, multi-layer	**Single layer:** Having one hidden layer. Example: single perceptron. **Multilayer:** Having multiple hidden layers. For example, multilayer perceptron.
Based on the nature of weights	Fixed, adaptive	**Fixed:** Weights are fixed a priori and not changed at all. **Adaptive:** Weights are updated and changed during training.
Based on memory unit	Static, dynamic	**Static:** Memory-less unit. The current output depends on the current input. For example, FeedForward network. **Dynamic:** Memory unit. The output depends on the current input as well as the current output. For example, RNN.

Neural network architecture types

Artificial Neural Network is the network that clones the functions of the human nervous system artificially. There are different types of artificial neural networks. These networks are developed using complicated mathematical functions and calculations which use a set of parameters to yield the output.

Here's a brief introduction of different kinds of neural networks:

- **Perceptron model in a neural network:** This type of system is considered to be the simplest type of neural network. It consists of one output unit and two input units with no hidden layers, thus it is also known as single-layer perceptrons.

- **Multilayer perceptron neural network:** The difference between the perceptron model and this model is that it has more than one hidden layer of neurons. For this reason, it is also known as deep feedforward neural network.

- **Radial basis function neural network:** These networks share most of the similarities with the feed-forward neural network. The significant difference is the use of radial basis function, which is used as the activation function of these neurons.

- **RNN:** This type of neural network consists of a self-connection between the neurons of the hidden layer. This functionality provides them a temporary memory. As a result, activation of the following value is forwarded from the lower layer as well as its previous activation value to the hidden layer neuron.

- **Long Short-Term Memory Neural Network (LSTM):** This is a subtype of a recurrent neural network. In it, the memory cell is embedded in the hidden layer neuron.

- **Hopfield network:** In this type of neural network, each neuron is connected with each of the other neurons, thus it is considered to be the fully connected network. A value of neurons to the desired pattern is fixed to train the system with input patterns. After that, the computation of weights takes place.

- **Boltzmann machine neural network:** This network shares the similarity with the Hopfield network; the significant difference is that some neurons are input whereas others are hidden in nature. In it, the initialization of the weights is a random process in which learning takes place using the backpropagation algorithm.

- **Modular Neural Network:** It is the combination of a structural type network that consists of different types of networks such as RNN, multilayer perceptron, Hopfield network, and other types of networks which are combined to form a single module.

- **Physical neural network:** This type of neural network ANN is adjusted electrically using resistance material to functionalize the synapse instead of any software simulations.

As mentioned earlier, there are so many similarities between the functioning of the human nervous system and artificial neural networks. There are different types of networks based on mathematical functions and set of parameters which are required to export the output. Some of the different kinds of neural networks are:

- **Neural network perceptron model:** These types of models have two input units and one output unit. In these networks, hidden layers are absent, thus they are also known as single-layer perceptrons.

- **Neural network based on radial basis function:** They share similarities with feed-forward neural networks except they have radial basis function, which is used as the activation function of these neurons.

- **Multilayer neural networks:** They are made of more than one layer of hidden neurons and also known as deep feedforward neural networks.

- **RNNs:** The advantage of these types of neural networks is that they have a unique ability to possess memory. These networks have this ability because of the interconnections between the neurons of the hidden layers. For this reason, they have to receive activation from the previous activation as well as from the lower activation function.

- **Long Short-Term Memory Neural Network:** This is a particular type of Recurrent Neural Network. In this network, a memory cell is situated under hidden neural networks.

- **Hopfield network:** These types of neural networks are considered to be fully connected, which implies that each neuron is fully connected to every other neuron. For training the system, the value of neurons is fixed according to a specific pattern on which neurons of input layers are trained. After that, weights are calculated. It is different from other neural networks

- **Boltzmann machine neural network:** These networks share similarities with the Hopfield network but have a very slight difference; some neurons are input, while others are considered to be hidden in nature. The backpropagation algorithm is used to provide learning and weights are initialized randomly.

- **Modular neural network:** These types of systems can be considered as a mixture of different kinds of neural networks such as Hopfield, RNNs, and other types of neural networks. These networks are moduled into a single network to perform different independent tasks.

- **Physical neural network:** These types of neural networks consist of electrically adjustable resistance material and used to emulate the synapse function in the place of any software simulations presented in neural networks.

The next figure talks about the different architecture of the neurons:

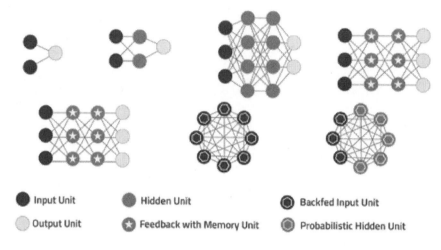

Figure 1.12: Different architecture types of neurons

Algorithmic problem-solving approach

In the previous sections, the basic concepts of deep learning, artificial intelligence, and their various applications were discussed. In this section, we will discuss an algorithmic approach to solve problems in a deep learning system with the deep learning algorithm. The following diagram shows a typical workflow for using deep learning in predictive modeling, which we will discuss in the following subsections:

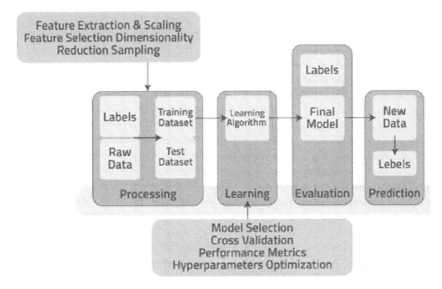

Figure 1.13: *Flow of the approach used for solving the problem with different steps*

Preprocessing

Raw data comes in various forms from multiple sources like IoT devices, social media, and health-care data. Most of the data is considered unstructured data. To get useful results from this unstructured data, there is a need to convert this data in such a form that can be used to make future predictions. At first, it must undergo Pre-processing that makes the data ready for further applications.

Let's take an example of the crack detection system in which there is a need to detect whether a plate is hot or not and also check if there is any crack in the dish. In the image dataset, the raw data consists of various images of plates and the requirement is to extract meaningful features.

Useful features can be the filename of the image, height, and width of an image, the name of the object, X and Y-coordinates of the purpose, the ID of the object, and so on (cracked areas).

Dimensionality reduction

While dealing with real-world problems and actual data, note that sometimes data is high dimensional with a million records. This high dimensionality of data can be reduced using one of the techniques, for example, **Principal Component Analysis (PCA).**

Scaling

Normalization is a scaling technique. It is also known as a mapping technique or a pre-processing stage. By using this, one can find the new range from an existing range. It can be beneficial for prediction or forecasting purposes. There are many ways to predict or forecast, but all can differ from each other. So, to keep the significant variation of prediction or forecasting, the normalization technique is required to make them closer.

Feature selection

The success of all the DL algorithms depends on how data is presented or whether the required features are extracted from the dataset. The following figure shows the various steps of feature extraction:

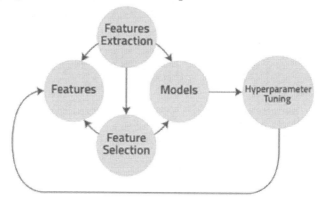

Figure 1.14: Different steps of Feature Extraction

Things to keep in mind while selecting features are as follows:

- Find covariance among the features and decide one out of likely related functions for the prediction.
- **Hyper-parameter features:** These features are created using a combination of two or more elements (the model performs operations to verify the received features; this process is repeated in a loop until the model gets satisfactory results).
- **Training and selecting a deep learning model:** As many deep learning models work based on availability, requirements, and form of data, to make an accurate prediction:
- There is a need to choose such a model that fits the data.
- It generalizes well to unseen data.

Now, the question that may come to your mind is how to find the most suitable and best-fitting model on available data and real-time data as well?

Model selection

The selection of an appropriate model for the problem is very significant to predict good results. Things to keepin mind while choosing any algorithms are as follows:

- **Accuracy:** To achieve better results from the model it is necessary to determine the extent of approximation of results of the obtained model. With this approach, the processing time increases. This approach also allows implementing the model by avoiding overfitting.

- **Training time:** The number of hours to train the model also plays a vital role in determining the selection of the model. It is directly related to the accuracy of the obtained model. On the other hand, some of the algorithms are dependent on the number of data points.

- **Linearity:** It is one of the assumptions which are followed while implementing the machine learning model. It states that a straight line can separate the classes.

- **Number of parameters:** It is the backbone of the model. The number of parameters affects the working of the model. Therefore, a large number of parameters for the model will require more time and trial to achieve an excellent combination of the model. The main advantage of having an optimized number of parameters is that it shows that the algorithm is very much flexible in a problematic point of view. It is also observed that with the use of an increased number of parameters, the requirement of time for training the model grows exponentially.

- **Number of features:** It is also considered in the decision of model selection. In some aspects, the number of features may be more extensive in number as compared to the number of data points. This can be observed in the case of textual datasets.

There are various algorithms that can be used for a particular type of task which are explained with the help of the following figures and some points after that. The following diagram representing the same:

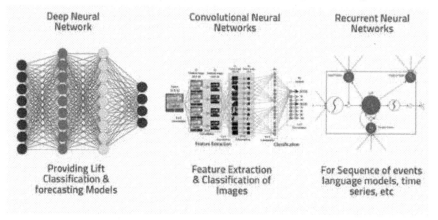

Figure 1.15: Different types of Networks with their different layers

- **Deep neural networks:** The deep neural network is helpful in classification and forecasting models.
- **Convolutional neural networks:** Convolutional neural network is used in feature extraction and image classification.
- **Recurrent neural network:** Recurrent neural network is helpful for a sequence of events and time series.

Cross-validation

It is a statistical method used to evaluate and compare learning algorithms by dividing the data into two segments: one used to learn or train a model, and the other set is used to validate the model.

For example, let's say someone wants to find a statistical model that predicts the price level of houses based on the previous day's prices. If one can achieve an accurate prediction based on that data, then it is easy to say that the model and feature selected for that task can generate actual results.

Using cross-validation, the user can estimate the test error of the particular learning method, and secondly, they can select the optimal flexibility of the chosen learning method to minimize the errors associated with bias and variance.

Performance metrics

Metrics are used to measure and compare the performance of algorithms. Various metrics such as confusion matrix and the area under the ROC curve can be used to check the accuracy of predicted results. (AUC — 0 ⇒ −ve , AUC −1 ⇒ +ve).

100% wrong .   100% correct .

Hyperparameter optimization

Hyperparameter is used to detect the approximate time required to train and test a model.

Evaluation of model and predicting patterns

After the selection of a model that fits well on the training dataset, the next step is to apply that model on the test dataset to predict patterns. If it generates satisfying results, the selected model can be used to predict new data.

For example, let's take the example of hot plates in which the objective is to detect whether the plate is hot or not and detect cracks in a plate. The dataset contains images of plates, and the task is to identify the area on a plate where there may be a crack:

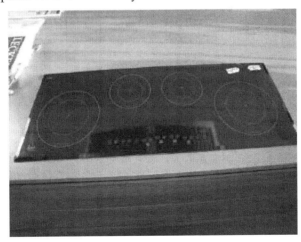

Figure 1.16: Real image of hot plate with crack

Various steps of collecting data are as follows.

Collection of data

1. The data is present in the form of .jpg images. Therefore, to detect the object from the image, there is a need to annotate the images, i.e. labeling the required object in the image so that the machine could learn which object has to be recognized.

2. Various tools are available to interpret images such as **Labellmg** and **Labelme**. To annotate in the form of the exact polygonal image we will use the Labelme tool, as the Labellmg tool is used to interpret the objects in the form of a rectangular box. For annotation, firstly open Labelme Annotation tool and log in the account. Then create the collection where the images are uploaded (maximum 20 images are uploaded at a time). Draw a polygonal boundary around the required object on the image. After drawing the boundary, name the label and save both .jpg and annotation files. Therefore, with the use of Labelme tool, images are interpreted and saved in the form of XML files.

3. After that, in order to fetch the points of the required detected object from images, the mask is generated using OpenCV to find contour function:

   ```
   ret,thresh = cv2.threshold(imgray,127,255,0)
   #setting the threshold value to classify the pixel
   values of the image
   im2, contours, hierarchy = cv2.
   findContours(thresh,cv2.RETR_TREE, cv2.CHAIN_APPROX_
   SIMPLE)
   #finding the white object from the black background
   #first one is the source image, second is the
   contour retrieval mode and third is the contour
   approximation method
   #get the result as a list of points in the form of
   list as "contours"
   ```

4. It is observed that the number of images is not sufficient for the implementation of object detection. Therefore, the number of images is increased with the use of data augmentation method. Many operations are available using the **Augmentor** Python library. Augmentor is a Python library to perform the augmentation and artificially generate image data for

machine learning and deep learning tasks. With the use of Augmentor Python library, the pipeline is developed by specifying operations. Execute the pipeline and save all the results in the specified path of the directory.

5. The few functions are as follows:

```
p.rotate(probability=0.7, max_left=10, max_right=10)
#rotating the image with probability 0.7 and maximum
movement towards left and right is 10
p.zoom(probability=0.5, min_factor=1.1, max_
factor=1.5)
#zooming the image with 0.5 probability within
certain range of factor
```

Preprocessing of data

1. From the above-obtained XML files, points are fetched using for loop and the received result is stored in the form of the CSV file.

2. After that, it is observed that object detection API does not work on polygonal points; it only works on the rectangular bounding box. Therefore, there is a need to convert polygonal points into the rectangular bounding box. It is performed using planar library and bounding box function. Here's an example:

```
for j in cor_list:
    bbox1 = BoundingBox(j)
# the points are listed in "cor_list" and
BoundingBox function is used to fetch points in the
form of rectangular box
    box_list_xmin.append(bbox1.min_point.x)
    box_list_ymin.append(bbox1.min_point.y)
    box_list_xmax.append(bbox1.max_point.x)
    box_list_ymax.append(bbox1.max_point.y)
#fetch the extreme points of x and y and append them
in the lists
```

3. Then, we observe that the information regarding image height and image width is missing, however, it is necessary for implementing an object detection module. Therefore, the PIL library is used to fetch it. The example is given as follows:

```
for xml_file in glob.glob(image_path + '/*.jpg'):
  xml_data = Image.open(xml_file)
```

```
size_image = list(xml_data.size)
value = size_image, os.path.basename(xml_file)
list.append(value)
```
```
#fetch all the jpg files from the given specified
using glob python library
#Open the fetched file
#fetch the height and width of the image using
"size" function of PIL python library
#store the name of the file with its image in a
variable and append them into the list
```

Preparation of data

1. After the preprocessing of data, it is split into train and test dataset in the ratio of 80% and 20%.

2. After that, both train and test dataset are converted into Tf.record file. Tf.record file is the format of the Tensorflow framework which it uses as input for training the model. Tf.record creates the bounding from points fetched on the image.

Training of data

First, install the object detection API of Tensorflow.

1. Make the directory named as data where models are downloaded:

   ```
   From tensorflow/models/research/
   mkdir data
   #command to create tfrecords
   ```

2. After making the directory, follow these instructions:

   1. Transfer the Train and Test tf.record files in the data directory.

   2. Transfer the Crack detection label file in the data directory.

   3. Make the directory named as new_crack_model where models are downloaded:

      ```
      #From tensorflow/models/research/
      mkdir new_crack_model
      ```

3. After making the directory, follow these instructions:

   1. Transfer the configuration file in the `new_crack_model` directory.

   2. Follow the *Step 3* and *4* of the main procedure.

   3. Make the directory named as `train` inside the `new_crack_model`.

      ```
      From tensorflow/models/research/
      mkdir train
      ```

4. After making the directory, follow these instructions:

   1. Transfer the `model.ckpt.data-00000-of-00001`, `model.ckpt.index` and `model.ckpt.meta` files from the `faster_rcnn_resnet101_coco_11_06_2017` pre-trained model to the `train` directory.

   2. Make the directory named as `eval` inside the `new_crack_model` directory:

      ```
      # From tensorflow/models/research/
      mkdir eval
      ```

Steps of implementation

- Set the paths in the given configuration file:
  - o Set the path for the initial checkpoint.
  - o Set the path for crack detection label file.
  - o Set the path for train record file.
  - o Set the path for Test record file.

- Start training the model using the following command:
  ```
  python object_detection/train.py \
  --logtostderr \
  --pipeline_config_path="path of configuration file" \
  --train_dir="path of train directory"
  ```

- Start the evaluation of the model simultaneously with the training of the model using the following command:
  ```
  #Test command
  Python object_detection/eval.py \
  --logtostderr \
  --pipeline_config_path="path of configuration file" \
  --checkpoint_dir="path of train directory" \
  ```

```
--eval_dir="path of eval directory"
```

- Visualize the results parallelly using the following command. The tensorboard (tool for visualization) command:

```
tensorboard --logdir="path of new_crack_model directory"
```

- Make the inference graph of the model after completing the training of the model using the following command. The command is given as follows:

```
python object_detection/export_inference_graph.py \
--input_type image_tensor \
--pipeline_config_path "path of configuration file" \
--trained_checkpoint_prefix "path of the checkpoint
obtained after training of the model" \
--output_directory "path of output file directory"
```

Testing of model

1. To test the obtained model, pass the path of the tested image and the path of obtained checkpoint while training.

2. While testing there is a feature to fetch the data on the basis of the score. Therefore, filtration of results can be implemented to achieve better and more accurate results. The example is given as follows:

```
if np.any(scores > 0.50):
    plt.figure(figsize=IMAGE_SIZE)
    plt.imshow(image_np1)
    plt.savefig('./crack_test_new9.svg')
```

Here, in the above example the score 0.50 is set and on the basis of that, the detection process is shown as output.

The output is displayed as shown in the following screenshot:

Figure 1.17: Detected crack in the image of hot plate

Conclusion

With the use of AI, the computing world has reached a different level of technology. New applications have cropped up to serve users with several customized and robust services that provide ease of work and ability to reduce risks in the future to a great extent. Data players are still doing a lot to obtain more from neural networks and automate things as much as possible. Therefore, there is no need to devise an algorithm to accomplish a specific task. Incorporating AI (ML, DL, NLP) in most of the areas are will do the job. These cutting edges are very well suited for real-time applications because of their quick response and fast computational processes arising from their parallel architecture and computation.

Neural networks are still under the scope of research work and also currently helping in other areas of research such as psychology and neurology. They are used to model parts of living organisms and to examine the internal mechanisms of the brain.

In order to get the best results, we need to integrate AI and fuzzy logic into computing and implement them in real-time business scenarios, as the AI is capable to formulate the best choices for us.

Questions

1. What is artificial intelligence? Please describe it briefly.

2. What is the role of data science, machine learning, and deep learning in the field of artificial intelligence?

3. What is deep learning?

4. What are the differences between machine learning and deep learning?

5. Please give a brief description of different types of neural networks. Please explain each of them briefly.

6. State all the steps involved in the process of deep learning. Explain each of them briefly.

CHAPTER 2
Data Science for Business Analysis

As the world is changing rapidly, it is resulting in changes in technologies. Due to such quick and major transformations, there is a lot to swallow for an enterprise and it's challenging to adopt new marketing channels like social media and web. Now, it is an entirely different process of decision making to choose to invest and utilize new technologies and compete on a global stage.

There are many disadvantages of such rapid pace of changes in the technological world; one of them is that no single employee or higher authority personnel can attain expertise over everything.

Structure

- Challenges faced during the business analysis of data science
- Problems that can occur during model development
- Discussions on artificial intelligence, deep learning, and machine learning

Objective

By the end of this chapter, we will learn to pursue business analysis from the perspective of data science. We will understand the different challenges, and different ways to design models with a glimpse of artificial intelligence, deep learning, and machine learning.

What is data science?

The term data science is commonly used in modern times, but what is the real meaning of data science? What are the main requirements to practice data science, and what are its main uses in the different fields of business? These are some questions that will be answered in this section.

Data science can be understood as a combination of various tools, algorithms, and machine learning techniques that emphasize on discovering patterns that are hidden in the layers of raw data.

It is an area of study that relies on the combination of expertise in domain, programming, math, and statistics; this combination is used to export substantial information from the data. Let us discuss some primary uses of data science.

Usage of data science:

- Data science can be used to develop high-precision risk assessment models for businesses; these models can be used to make the business robust.

- In the area of automobiles, deep learning can be used to record audio signals from the engine, and the data can be further used to determine whether the engine requires any maintenance. This is known as *predictive analytics*.

- In the area of health care, with the help of predictive analytics and prescriptive analytics, not only prediction of diseases is possible, but remedial measures can also be prescribed.

These are a few business cases that show how data science can be used in solving the different problems of businesses. Now let us see what the main challenges faced by businesses are.

Challenges faced by businesses

Some of the most significant challenges businesses faces today are uncertainty, globalization, innovation, government policy and regulation, diversity, complexity, technology, supply chains, strategic thinking and problem solving, and information overload. The following diagram illustrates the challenges faced by businesses:

Figure 2.1: *Challenges faced by businesses*

Uncertainty

A small business faces a wide variety of challenges. Besides handling issues of employees, sustaining the quality of product or service, and keeping the wealth flows positive, administrators get stretched in multiple directions. The most delicate part of business management is that it's difficult to know in advance what comes up next. Therefore, uncertainty is one of the most critical issues faced by small enterprises. The types of risks faced by small businesses are as follows:

- **State uncertainty:** It is a situation where a business manager is unable to visualize the results of a particular business environment. For example, if you are running a business that is managed mostly outdoors, then changes in weather can also cause uncertainty. It can also get affected by government policies that are favorable for your business.

- **Effect uncertainty:** Effect uncertainty is a condition when someone cannot foresee the effects of external events on your business in the near future. For example, in an outdoor business, you know that it is going to rain, but you don't know its effects on your customers.

- **Response uncertainty:** To counter the effects of change you can plan a response. However, this is where response uncertainty comes in. It is the inability to be sure of market reaction to your responses. For example, if you move your business from outdoors to indoors, you can't be sure that your customers will respond well.

Globalization

Globalization is the functioning of a business on a global level. When you practice trade from a place different than your local market, you globalize your business. Usually, there are specific barriers when it comes to the functioning of a company on an international platform. These barriers may be political, financial, or even geographical. When a business overcomes such barriers, it is called a global industry. Of course, these businesses are profit-oriented and have an utterly functional base apart from the one in their local market. The factors affecting globalization are mentioned below:

- **Increased competition:** Globalization leads to a surge in competition. This competition can be related to product, market, technology, services, and more. Customers have a vast magnitude of choices in the market which affects their behaviors; they want to buy goods quickly and more efficiently than before. Also, they expect high quality and low prices. To fulfill these requirements, a response is required from companies. Thus, a company must always be flexible toward price, product, service, and customer preferences because all of these are global market requirements.

- **Greater awareness and reactions to customer needs:** Due to the rise of social media and the web, now consumers seem to be very cautious about the quality, price, and service.

- **Economies related to the different scales:** Sale of products across different countries and continents resulting in increasing competition among companies with large-scale production.

- **Location flexibility:** With advancements in techniques and technologies, service provisions can be allocated almost anywhere, this allows gaining the advantages of low-cost labor and other resource charges.

- **Increased mergers and joint ventures:** Globalization allows access to more significant markets and associated cost advantages.
- **Economies of scale:** Nowadays, products or services can sell across many continents, thus businesses can enter markets with large populations, which makes them very competitive.

Innovation

It is one of the problems faced by organizations. Many organizations are not open to change. Innovation is one of the renewing processes of the organization. It is one of the refreshing methods carried out by organizations such as rebranding, launching new products and services, and many more. The innovation process consists of four key points such as searching, selecting, implementing, and capturing value by analyzing the purpose of the knowledge gathered during the information creation process.

Government policy and regulation

Government policies play an essential role in the decision making process of an organization. Therefore, data science can help us examine and finalize the resources for building systems. Many financial and environmental policies are complicating the decision process of companies. Therefore, there is a need to understand the procedures in the industry and how they can be implemented appropriately for the corresponding business.

Diversity

Diversity is observing the views of the people. Therefore, this particular factor becomes a challenge as many people do not agree with each other's opinions. Further, disagreements make it challenging to run the business successfully. Lack of diversity among people also leads to the lack of different views of a changing world and the trends of technologies. To handle this, a proper variety among people should be defined in the organization so that different creative ideas can be expanded while maintaining the environment in the organization.

Complexity

The global economy is expanding day by day due to the availability of more diverse people, that is, customers and suppliers. The IT industry is also becoming flexible, and service providers are taking advantage of them. Therefore, systems to provide the required services are getting complex. Thus, to build the system correctly and deliver the requirements better, there is a need to make the system in such a way that unnecessary complexity of the improved method can be removed. Less complex systems with better thinking capability will provide the required results.

Technology

As technology is changing at a fast rate, businesses face many challenges in daily operations. Some of them are mentioned below:

- **Outdated hardware/software:** In today's fast-changing business world, hardware and software become obsolete very fast. One solution to this problem is to use standardized software applications and hardware.

- **Illegal or pirated software:** Due to ignorance, sometimes companies end up using illicit or pirated software. They have to pay millions of dollars to software manufacturers as fine if they are caught doing so.

- **Lack of control over employee devices:** To prevent the devices of employees being used for illegal purposes is a significant problem. Usually, employees bring their own devices like pen drives to the companies and leak the confidential material of the office. Companies need to take strict actions to control sensitive data and prevent data theft.

- **Integration issues:** Sometimes, small-scale companies purchase the latest software applications without proper planning. They miss out on asking questions such as whether this software can integrate with the existing systems? As a result, there is a waste of time and money to find out how to incorporate software into the system.

Supply chains

The core of business operations is where the supply chain lies; here, managers have to tackle various issues daily due to which companies gets affected. The two most prominent issues which affect supply chain managers are the management of inventory and management of suppliers. Supply chain managers are the ones who acquire the knowledge of the number of suppliers required, the procedure of receiving orders, and delivering the product on time. Thus, there is a need for proper management of the inventory and ensuring sufficient stock so that the expectations of all customers are met.

Strategic thinking and problem solving

Problem-solving and critical thinking refers to the ability to use knowledge, facts, and data to solve problems efficiently. It doesn't mean you need to have an immediate answer; it means you have to be able to think, assess issues, and find solutions. The ability to develop a well-thought solution within a reasonable time frame is a skill that employers value greatly. In a company, employers want employees who can work through problems on their own, have creative thinking, share thoughts and opinions, and make decisions. It helps in saving time, effort, and money.

Information overload

Information overload refers to an overabundance of information, which is a significant cause of concern for general information users, researchers, and information managers. In today's world, with rapid technological changes, the rate of information production has overgrown. Due to this, it's tough for people to find the required information quickly and efficiently from various online sources. At a certain point, the data received by decision-makers exceed the limits they can process, and that's how information overload occurs, and the ability of decision-making decreases.

Problems that occur during model development

From the above section, we've got answers for questions like *What is data science?, How it can be used in different business fields?,* and *What are the main challenges before businesses that should be tackled with the help of data science?* These models act as the backbone of any product and service. Models can be developed using different techniques such as machine learning and deep learning, but the soul of their development process remains constant. Let us look at their design and development process and the main problems that can occur during the development of the model.

Design and development of models

While planning on producing a new product and service, the critical factor is designing the model. To make designs successful, there is a need to follow some basic principles like the refinement of existing products, translation of customers' wants and needs, development of new products and services, formulation of quality goals, and formulation of cost targets. The process of design has some steps that include motivation, ideas for improvement, organizational capabilities, and forecasting.

Technological changes, the competitive market, and economic and demographic changes are some opportunities and threats that organizations must be aware of while planning a product and service design. While designing a new product, businesses must take into account environmental and legal concerns as well.

The overall development process of the model is divided into six phases that are shown in the following diagram:

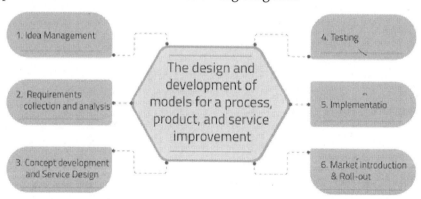

Figure 2.2: Overall development process of models is divided into six phases

The six phases shown in the preceding diagram are explained below:

- **Idea management:** Analysis and assessment of the idea together constitute the first step in the service development process. It is initialized with the collection of ideas considering specific services. The next step is to clean the idea to generate a pattern. Generally, the elaboration of preliminary concepts is used for suitable service ideas.

- **Requirements collection and analysis:** The second phase is the process of analyzing the requirements for developing the project. Requirements coming from different stakeholders are recorded, analyzed, and compared. These observations are used to demonstrate the initial point for elaborated planning of the recurrent service.

- **Service design and concept development:** Conceptualization can be considered as the third phase: service definition, organizational concept, and the marketing concept. The initial target of this phase is to elaborate the services in a vast, manner, which can then be used to define the parameters of the organization and planning resources deployment. The conceptualization phase also helps to elaborate on a marketing concept to enable market and customer aspects that are relevant to the future market trends to be taken into account at an early stage of the development process.

- **Testing:** After the development of the concept, the next step is to test the accuracy and efficiency of the product. Several tests need to be done on the product such as the usability test and the conceptual test, explained below:
  - o Usability tests are used to check the operating resources like hardware and software. It is possible to measure the user-friendliness of these resources by applying test methods derived from usability engineering.
  - o Conceptual tests are used to verify the consistency of the service documentation like business plans, process models, and more. However, the question here is whether or not the company's employees and clients can handle the new resources.

- **Implementation:** The implementation phase follows testing; in other words, the conceptualization and testing work that is carried out in the earlier steps is implemented in the company in this phase. It also includes effective implementation of the previously elaborated marketing concept.

- **Market introduction and roll-out:** The market launch phase for new services, or say, software mainly consists of internal and external communication and information measures. After the development of the software or product, this phase also helps to monitor the accuracy and efficiency of the product. The product is finally adaptable only after proper feedback is received from the marketplace, customers, and employees.

Today, innovations play an important role. Only those businesses are thriving that invest in innovation and research. Managing innovation activities in the market is necessary. But, there is a need for companies to bring new products, innovative ideas, and services to the market. If the firms do not upgrade their products, the products will become unattractive, and they would have to close down the firm, which is not the goal of any entrepreneur.

The main aim is to acquire new knowledge in the field of innovation management and to focus on the area of innovation strategies. The next aim is to highlight the possibility of creating models for creating an innovation strategy in a business that guarantees its successful implementation. It can identify the main problems that hinder the implementation of innovation strategy in a business successfully and provide appropriate recommendations.

Problems faced by IT organizations while developing models

Various issues crop up in the formulation and implementation of an innovation strategy to develop models in the business. Firstly, to define the difficulty diagnosing the solution is required to focus better on the problem. Various techniques are available to recognize the exact process to identify and analyze the problem. Different vital steps need to be implemented for defining the problem, such as the participation of interested candidates and focus on the cause of the described problem.

Some of the problems regarding IT organizations are described below:

- **Inappropriate preparation of innovative program:** Improper development of the innovative program is a problem in implementing an innovation strategy in the business. The company must have sufficient details about creative processes and innovative capacity, resources, and information flows for the successful realization of an innovation strategy. If corporations do not pay the necessary attention to this work and develop innovation strategies by sufficient documentation, then the innovation plan can fail. Business managers can be recommended to carry out a detailed analysis of the current situation and correctly understand the role of technology in implementing the innovation strategy.

- **Automation of processes:** In some cases, there is a need to automate the previously erroneous innovative processes. Business managers need to identify and continuously update the innovation processes. There is a need to emphasize on methods that are directly related to the work of change and recognizing the missing ways.

- **Lack of proof of innovative ideas:** Another problem is the absence of evidence of creative ideas, opportunities, and innovations. Marketing managers have no idea of the invention coming from the external or internal environment. Business managers can use IT applications for gathering and storing essential data in a standard database. It is also a fact that failures come while diagnosing the strategic goals. The primary problems while determining purposes are that there is no clarity of the benefits of innovation policies, there is a lack of understanding about them in the organization, and how these innovations are applied in the applications. The steps that are recommended are given below:

  o Proper understanding of the problem is needed by examining the literature survey and obtaining appropriate advice from a professional person.

  o Adequate clarification of the issue should be there by implementing innovation strategies.

  o The entire organization should focus on a shared vision.

- **The improper starting point of formulated strategy:** Most of the time, a situation occurs when the business decides to implement something innovative. Still, the fact is not apparent that form the basis for formulating a change strategy. The critical success factors are to ensure the fulfillment of business needs with business goals. Recently, the role of the customer has increased in developing the processes for business strategy. Their requirements, expectations, and desires are directly or indirectly linked to the form of business goals. When a business chooses a starting point to create and formulate an innovation strategy, the business strategy will ensure a sufficient knowledge base for the development of innovation strategy. Business managers can be recommended to review the business goals about its desired innovative direction and projection of innovations into long-term business plans.

- **Prohibition of human factors:** The problem observed in this phase is that the employees are less indulged in the development and making of innovation strategies for the organization. Therefore, the following points are recommended:

    o Regular communication between the employees in the organization should be maintained.

    o Employees should be able to participate in the development of the innovation strategy.

    o Creative ideas should be welcomed and considered while making plans.

    o The importance of the strategy of the organization should be explained to the employees.

- **Absence of feedback:** While setting measurable goals for a company, the management can assess and evaluate the benefits of the implementation of innovative strategies. A prevalent problem in the process of implementing a policy is the absence of feedback. It is essential that the whole process of creating change in the approach is to analyze from the beginning to the end of the implementation with continuous monitoring. Business managers can be recommended to follow some defined rules like:

    o Main priorities set the metrics in the management of innovative business activities.

    o Need to identify goals of introducing innovation strategy and measurable indicators.

    o Selection of appropriate parameters to assess the fulfillment of established goals.

- **Non-utilization of innovation strategies:** The main problem arises when misunderstanding happen among employees. Consequently, the process is implemented inefficiently.

Artificial intelligence and deep learning methods to develop models

Artificial intelligence(AI) has become the focus of business due to a significant increase in investments and adaptiveness concerning the enterprise level. With the use of AI, it becomes possible to make the machine learn from previous experiences. After learning, the device can adjust as per the new environment and perform the task like a human would. Most of the examples of AI belong to automation, such as self-driving cars that work on DL models, and NLP. With the use of technologies mentioned above, machines can work on specific tasks with the use of a significant amount of data and recognize different patterns from it.

Artificial intelligence (AI)

Artificial intelligence (AI) had arrived in the year 1956. At that time, it mainly focused on problem-solving and symbolic methods. After a few years, it started exploring some human-like basic reasoning by training machines. With time, the use of AI and advancements went on increasing. Finally, in the 20th century, it started working on decision support systems and smart search systems. These systems were designed to enhance human abilities. In the future, maybe AI-based robots will be able to change evolution.

The following are the usage of AI:

- **AI helps in the automation of repetitive learning and discovery using data:** It works reliably and without fatigue to perform everyday computerized tasks with high volumes. That said, even for the machines to be set up and work perfectly, the involvement of human beings is required.

- **Addition of human intelligence:** AI can be used in existing products as well. Rather than focusing on new working projects, it can contribute to increasing the intelligence level of the machine. Collectively many fields such as automated smart machines and bots with a significant amount of data can work together to improve the security intelligence of the current device.

- **Adaption using progressive learning algorithms:** AI helps in finding structure and regularities from the data so that the algorithm can adapt to the required skills. For example, as the algorithm can teach itself to play games, in the same way, it can learn which product or service it should recommend to the customer. Therefore, the model will reorganize whenever any new data is obtained. To do this, an algorithm of AI is used, which is known as back propagation. This allows the model to learn by training and adapt to the new environment when new data is given.

- **The ability to analyze more in-depth data:** Incredible changes are observed in the field of AI through increasing computer power and big data. Let's say if there is a need to detect fraud from the data, it is not possible or feasible to use traditional ML techniques with few hidden layers and get better results. Therefore, DL models are preferred. But, DL models require a large amount of data as they train by using data directly. More the data, the more the accuracy of the model.

Deep learning (DL)

Deep learning (DL) belongs to a family of AI techniques whose models extract essential features from the data and find meaningful patterns in the dataset. Unlike traditional methods in which the developer of the model has to choose and encode features ahead of time, DL enables a model to learn features automatically. In this way, a DL model determines a representation of the data, making deep learning part of the larger field of representation learning.

DL is a technique that helps us develop models that can be the backbone of different AI solutions— solutions that can be used in driverless cars, enabling them to recognize signs and potholes. Deep learning models can also be used to develop an AI solution that can provide virtual voice assistants in different devices like phones, tablets, TVs, and hands-free speakers. DL is achieving results that were not possible earlier.

In practice, DL models require millions of iterations of training, which can take several hours to complete. It depends on the number of weights in the network and the difficulty of the task. Similarly, a considerable amount of training data is necessary to get excellent performance, because this training data must contain all the details, nuances, structural patterns, and sources of error that could be present in any input. For example, to recognize photos of animals that are taken from a variety of angels, it needs to be shown images from those angles during training. Depending on the task, this contains thousands to millions of data points, occupying gigabytes or terabytes of storage.

Why DL matters?

DL attains impressive results. Regarding accuracy, deep learning achieves recognition accuracy at higher levels than before. Recent advances in DL outperform humans in various tasks like the classification of objects in images. It was first introduced in the 1980s, but it became useful recently because of two main reasons:

- DL requires amounts of labeled data. For example, the classification of animals requires millions of images.

- DL requires high computing power. High-performance GPUs that have a parallel architecture are efficient for deep learning. When combined with clusters or cloud computing, the training time for models is reduced from weeks to hours or less.

Usage of deep learning

There are many use cases of deep learning which can be used for business analysis:

- Deep learning models can be trained on call details and records, trading activities, point of sale transactions, and more. These models can be used for fraud analysis i.e. identifying activities that are likely to be a fraud.

- Deep learning models can also be used for risk analysis, which is a way to understand and then predict risks before the next market crisis.

- Deep learning algorithms with the combination of regression can be used to find real-time anomalies, which are more specific pattern analysis.

Improvements in the business

Professionals from various disciplines in the field of healthcare, retail, and financial services industries are going for data-driven decision-making. More businesses are turning towards artificial intelligence to improve the efficiency of the products. Deep learning is emerging as a critical focus area for AI researchers, developers, and investors alike, due to its many potential applications. This sub-category of AI moves from creating rule-based systems to the development of algorithms that can be trained to learn from data and identify patterns and insights automatically from experience.

AI and DL are impacting many areas of our lives with tools such as Google Maps, which help us with locations and interact with other applications to give us online recommendations.

Due to the complexity and large size of the datasets, deep learning can help us find value in the data; this is something that humans cannot do. As a result, DL is now able to make better business decisions and more reasonable courses of action with minimal human intervention.

DL to optimize manufacturing

Product optimization is a big issue in many organizations recently. Optimization is required in any act, process, or methodology that makes something like design, system, or decision. Decision processes with minimal cost, better quality, performance, and consumption of energy are examples of such optimization.

Global companies currently focus on digitization and analytics. The focus is to analyze the vast amounts of data that are accumulated from thousands of sensors every day. Until recently, proper utilization of such data was limited due to the lack of necessary technology and data pipelines for collecting data from sensors and systems for further analysis.

Oil and gas production is a complicated process, and lots of necessary decisions must be taken to meet long-term goals, starting from planning and asset management to corrective actions. Short-term actions have to be made within a limited time, which is characterized as daily production optimization. They seek to maximize the rate of oil and gas production by optimizing various parameters that control the production process.

To handle issues related to manufacturing, the use of an in-depth learning-based approach becomes helpful. So far, the optimization performed by experts manually is by their own experience and familiarity with controlling the processing. This ability of experts to learn from previous experience is similar to a technology called DL. By analyzing vast amounts of historical data from several IoT devices, the deep learning algorithms can learn and understand relations between parameters and their effects on the production.

Time series analysis for business forecasting

Time is the only moving thing in the world that never stops. When it comes to forecasting, the human mind tends to be more curious as we know that things change with time. Hence, a businessman is always interested in making predictions ahead of time. In the cases where time is an influencing factor, there will be so many other potentially valuable factors which can be considered as predictable.

So here, we are going to discuss time series forecasting. The name, time-series, itself suggests that data related to it varies with time.

The primary motive of time series problems is forecasting. Time series analysis for business forecasting helps to forecast/predict the future values of a critical field that has a potential business value in the industry, predict the health condition of a person, the result of a sport, or performance parameters of a player based on previous performances and data.

Various time-series methods that can help to improve business are:

- Univariate time series forecasting
- Multivariate time series forecasting

A univariate time series forecasting problem has only two variables. One is date-time, and the other is the field that is needed to be forecasted. For example, if someone wants to predict a particular weather field like average temperature for tomorrow, there is a need to consider the temperatures of all the previous dates and use them in the model to predict for tomorrow.

In the multivariate case, the target would be the same, let's consider the above example as univariate, the goal is identical i.e. to predict average temperature for tomorrow, but the difference is that we can use other parameters also that affect the temperature. If there's a chance for rainfall, then we need to consider the duration of the rain, the wind speed at different times, humidity, atmospheric pressure, precipitation, solar radiation, and many more.

All these factors are intuitively relevant to temperature. The primary point of consideration in comparison for univariate and multivariate is that multivariate is more suited for practical scenarios.

DL in bot recommendation

Autobot recommendation is a recommendation platform that can be developed using a set of algorithms and techniques designed to use the data and generate output depending on the data and requirements. In any industry or business, they try to focus on retaining their old customers and getting new customers. They may want to recommend offers to make new customers, or they may need a recommender system for their customers that'll help them in and exploring and shopping products, keeping customers' historical information into consideration.

The advantage of DL-based autobots is that they keep a customer's preferences as their priority. Since not all products are long-lasting, there will be a change in trends and variations in the interests of people. One cannot keep track of these details across hundreds of products in the market to get the maximum profit. With all other various techniques, it also helps industrialists do market basket analysis for a particular industry to keep an eye on the product's demand and rating.

If we consider a shopping mall or a retail store, the store owner requires various types of suggestions like where should be the placement of a product or combination of products to run. For this, the data for the analysis could be transaction data. Based on the transactions done by the customers, we can find out the following details:

- Which products are more likely to be sold and are in high demand in that area and providing maximum profits?
- What the products often bought together?

Platforms like autobots give recommendations in real-time and are designed to work in many industries like music, retail, banking, movies, people, interactive sites, and so on. It profoundly analyses patterns in behavior in its every task, and it's made in such a way that it tracks everything, from logged-in customers, online/offline customers to which product they viewed. It gives recommendations on streaming data also after running models on historical data.

Predictive and preventive maintenance for industrial IoT

Predictive maintenance is essential in diverse application areas, such as manufacturing industry, information technology, aerospace, heavy-machinery sector, and so on, to estimate the future performance of a subsystem or a component to make **Remaining Useful Life (RUL)** estimation. If one can accurately predict when an asset (which may be any machine, a server, or a turbine) will fail, then one can make planned maintenance decisions in advance to avoid sudden failures, reduce the maintenance cost, as well as streamline operational activities.

This may seem a bit theoretical, but this is feasible using modern-day data technologies. We can monitor our assets (can be any device or machine that may lead to breakdown) in real-time via sensors, and based on the sensor data patterns, we can predict when we are going to have a break-down of those assets.

Preventive maintenance is the maintenance that is performed regularly on a piece of equipment to reduce the possibility of it breaking down or increasing the lifetime of the stuff. Such maintenance is scheduled based on the usage or on time elapsed since last support. A typical example of time-based preventive maintenance is an air conditioner that is serviced every year before the summer starts. Preventive maintenance is a primitive method of maintaining that is costly because we cannot predict the remaining useful life of an asset or equipment. We do maintenance check-ups regularly based on usage or time elapsed from the last check-up, even if the maintenance is not at all needed.

Here the concept of predictive analytics comes in. Using IoT and DL, we can predict when an asset is going to break down, thereby enabling us to perform a maintenance check on the affected parts when necessary.

Merits of predictive maintenance over preventive maintenance practices are as follows:

- Predictive maintenance helps in identifying key parameters and determining the likelihood of breakdowns.
- Predictive maintenance helps in optimizing business decision-making, systematically using real-time and old relevant data.
- It helps in better planning of spare inventory so that the inventory or maintenance team doesn't face phases of pressure.

Deep learning in security

Cybercriminals continue to launch increasingly sophisticated attacks on industries, businesses, and financial organizations around the world. It is clear that organizations cannot merely rely on workforce and human capabilities to fight cyberattacks since it is very time consuming to find potential threats and to come up with security technologies to prevent them.

As a result, companies have to find new ways to boost their cyber defenses. AI is emerging as the technology that can battle against cybercrime. Cybersecurity experts need a reliable way to scan, parse, and react to anomalies quickly. Once ML, DL, and AI learn what to look for, they can promptly give their human counterparts, the information they need to mitigate attacks and the fallout.

AI can help businesses make better decisions by analyzing threats and respond immediately to attacks and security incidents. It also helps to automate tasks that were previously carried out by under-skilled security teams. It allows engineers to figure out the approach to find an attack, learn the intricacies of the work, and apply those lessons to future attacks. This means the technology can use those lessons to stop an attack or alert a human operator to respond to an incident that can shorten the response time and lessen the financial and reputational damage from a customer-facing hack.

Deep learning in healthcare

In the present era, patients' expectations are changing as they are now more demanding with healthcare providers. Busy schedules and rising costs of treatments make it difficult for many people to make and keep doctor's appointments.

Patients accustomed to mobile devices want the same choices during their healthcare interactions. Service providers are dealing with the multiple health-related concerns of an aging population, and it has become challenging to collaborate with health-care teams and coordinate treatment plans. Even as privacy concerns and regulations have made managing patient information more complicated, the explosion of electronic health records and mobile devices in healthcare has led to new and expanding security risks.

Of course, cost pressures are at the top of the mind for almost every patient and provider today. As payers increase their focus on outcomes and quality, health care providers must find some ways to improve patient experience, reduce costs, thereby increasing the productivity of work.

Fraud detection with deep learning neural network

Banks have to analyze millions of money transactions in a day. But due to the lack of advanced techniques, banks are not able to examine transactions properly as it becomes challenging to identify a few fraud activities within millions of transactions. Therefore, a scalable technique is needed, which updates the system automatically. Deep learning neural networks can detect fraud activities automatically, and the system can learn automatically whenever new data arrives without the interference of a human being.

Larger institutions and organizations indulge in significant financial transactions. So, open-source-DL is introduced for them to fight fraudulent activities at economical rates.

Benefits of data science in business analysis

Data science and AI are revolutionizing every field and area nowadays. Let us discuss what benefits are offered by data science in the area of business analysis:

- Data science provides predictive analytics which can be used to predict the needs as well as risks involved in any business, which results in an increase in proactivity and anticipation.

- Using predictive analytics and prescriptive analytics, all the errors can be tackled or avoided, which results in the delivery of the relevant products.

- Data science can also be used to develop recommendation systems and sentiment analysis systems that can be used for personalization and services.

- Data science techniques and models can also be used for optimizing and improving operational efficiency.

Conclusion

In this chapter, we discussed decision-making by observing different elements and models that are important to every decision.

Uncertainty is complicated and it has not been made specific in any decision support system yet. One task which is essential for regulating the decision support system is interpreting the operational decision.

With the precise analysis of uncertainties, attitude towards uncertainty may be derived. So, it can be said that attitudes towards risk in decision making is a vital decision itself and should not be left for individual decision-makers if a consistent and rational operation is to be achieved.

Questions

1. What are the main challenges of business? Explain each of them briefly.

2. Explain the development process of models and its phases briefly.

3. Explain some problems faced by IT organizations.

4. Explain some applications of DL in IT organizations.

5. Briefly explain the importance of DL.

CHAPTER 3
Decision Making

Knowledge is a necessity of intelligent behavior. Without knowledge, an agent won't be able to make informed decisions and will instead rely on using some form of exploration and communication, to gain missing knowledge. Humans depend on knowledge at every moment of their lives in many ways, such as how to communicate with other humans, how to behave in stressful situations, or how to perform different tasks. Without the human ability to store and process knowledge, their capabilities are severely diminished.

Structure

- This chapter starts by discussing the different ways to represent a problem and moved ahead with more discussions on algorithms.
- We'll discuss design and development, knowledge representation, and reasoning.
- We'll discuss different techniques of knowledge representation.

- Finally, all the findings of this chapter are discussed by taking an example of a use case related to Uber.

Objective

The prime objective of this chapter is to discuss different ways of knowledge representation and to discuss the different ways of using knowledge in decision making.

Representation of problems

After identifying a problem, there is a need to take the time to represent it. Representation of a problem may involve thinking abstractly, but it can also include putting the problem in a tangible form. Let us discuss the different aspects of representation of problems.

> **Use a roadmap when representing the solution of a problem and identify the long-term issues.**

A human mind is able to focus on only a small amount of information at a time, and it becomes complicated to hold a detailed picture of a problem in our minds. Without this, we may overlook essential relationships.

The best solution is to make a roadmap in which we decide the plan that is associated with ideas and concepts in our minds, forming patterns that are learned by experience. Information that is new or seems unlikely and plans that appear irrelevant may be either excluded or not get retained in memory because of their weak associations with the problem.

Artificial intelligence models give structure and shape to information and make it easy to remember, comprehend, and build on our ideas. They can also highlight gaps in collected details, help to predict the consequences of our planned actions, and stimulate the senses. AI models give ideas for better solutions to people.

Many problem-solving tasks can be developed in a state space. A state space consists of various states of the domain and a set of operators that can change from one state to another.

The rules can be described as nodes in a connected graph and the operators as edges. Individual nodes are represented as destination nodes, and a problem is said to be solved when a path is found from the initial state to a destination state. State spaces can get various search methods that control the search efficiency appropriately.

To solve a problem, the strategy that should be followed is described with the following steps:

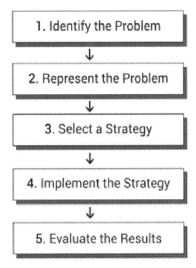

Figure 3.1: *Steps to solve a problem*

The following steps can be followed to resolve a problem:

1. **Identify the problem:** Identifying a problem is the most challenging task of problem-solving because of the obstacles that need to be overcome. When looking back, a challenge and a solution may seem obvious, but that does not mean they were apparent at the beginning. To identify the problem, the following obstacles should be overcome:

   • **A detailed search for a problem:** To identify any problem, one has to go into the depths of the problem. A detailed search of the problem is required to overcome the challenges.

   • **Relevant background knowledge:** To identify a problem, one must be familiar with the topic of research.

   • **Take time to reflect on the problem:** Expert problem-solvers spend significantly more time thinking about the problem compared to amateurs and do not give up when the going gets tough. They do not view problem-solving as a time-limited activity.

- **Think divergently:** Divergent thinking means to think at a broader level and look at problems in new ways. Try to avoid solutions that may not seem to match the challenge.

2. **Represent the problem:** Some problems have a limited number of possible solutions while continuing problems can usually be solved in a large number of ways. The most effective solution for analyzing a problem involves the identification and collection of relevant information and representing it in a meaningful way. A detailed analysis of the problem helps to identify all the possible causes and confirm the real reason.

3. **Select a strategy:** Several possible strategies may be used to solve a problem such as algorithms, heuristics, trial and error, and so on.

   - **Algorithms:** An algorithm is defined as a set of step-by-step procedures that provide the correct answer to a particular problem. The use of an algorithm helps to solve a problem or make a decision that yields the best possible solution. Algorithms are used in such a situation where accuracy is critical or where similar types of problems need to be solved frequently. In such cases, computer programs are designed to speed up this process. Data needs to be placed in the system so that the algorithm can be executed to come up with the correct solution. Such step-by-step approaches of algorithms can be useful in situations where each decision must follow the same process and where accuracy is critical. Because the process follows a prescribed procedure, one can be sure that they will reach the correct answer every time.

   - **Heuristics:** A heuristic is a mental shortcut method that allows people to make judgments and solve problems quickly. Our past experiences typically form these mental shortcuts and enable us to act quickly. However, heuristics are more of a rule of thumb; they don't always guarantee a correct solution. For instance, a physician, while deciding to treat a patient, could use an algorithm approach. But this would be a very time-consuming task, and patients need treatment immediately. In this case, the doctor would rely on their expertise and past experiences to promptly choose the right treatment method. Another instance, suppose a customer purchases three items at a store at these prices— *$9.95, $29.98,* and *$39.97.* Now, if one is to calculate the total amount of money spent. The fastest way to do this is to round off the prices. Thus, the first item costs about *$10,* the second about *$30,* and the third about *$40;* therefore, the customer spent about *$80* on shopping. Rounding off is an excellent heuristic for quickly arriving at approximate answers to mathematical problems. Problem-solving algorithms and heuristics are specific to the particular type of problem domain. But there are several general problem-solving heuristics that are helpful in a variety of contexts:

- o **Identify the subgoals:** By breaking a large and complex task into two or more specific subtasks, it can be easier to complete.

- o **Jot down points:** Draw a diagram; list a problem's components; or jot down important points, potential solutions, and approaches.

- o **Draw an analogy:** Determine an analogous situation and derive potential solutions from the analogy.

- o **Brainstorm:** Generate a variety of different possible approaches or solutions. Once a list of approaches or solutions has been created, evaluate them for their potential relevance and usefulness.

- o **Incubate the situation:** Suppose a problem remains unresolved for a few hours or days. In this case, we must allow some time for a broader search for productive approaches.

- **Trial and error:** A technique called trial and error can solve some complex problems. Trial and error are typically good for issues where a user has multiple chances to get the correct solution. However, this is not a proper technique for problems that don't give you numerous opportunities to find a solution.

For instance, trial and error is not useful in situations such as defusing a bomb, or while operating on a patient. In these situations, a small failure can lead to a disaster.

Trial and error is used best when it is applied to cases that give the user a sufficient amount of time and safety to come up with a solution.The trial and error method is not considered the best method of finding a solution, nor is it a method for detecting all possible solutions. It is just a problem-solving technique that is used merely to find a solution. One of the advantages of this technique is that it does not require the user to have a lot of knowledge. However, it may require a significant amount of patience. Trial and error is typically used to discover new drugs, and it also play san essential role in many scientific methods.

- **Implementing the strategy:** Taking a decision and making a decision aretwo different things. After carefully planning the project, the next step is to start the project implementation i.e. the fourth phase of the project management. The implementation phase involves putting the project plan into action. A process needs to be followed to accelerate the ability to learn and implement an algorithm manually from scratch. The more the algorithms you apply, the faster and more efficiently will you achieve results.

4. **Accuracy:** During this phase, the automated system/ application and IT solution move towards the production status. The process of implementation depends on the characteristics of the project and the IT solution. If necessary, data needs to be converted and trained for use. The operations and maintenance of the system are also done during this phase. From a security perspective, the system must be certified in the production environment during the implementation phase. The following steps need to be considered during implementation:

   - **Select the programming language:** Select the programming language that the user wants to use for the implementation. This decision will be implemented using APIs and standard libraries during deployment.

   - **Select algorithm:** The algorithm that you want to implement from scratch needs to be selected. Try to be as specific as possible, meaning always choose a particular description or implementation that you want to implement, along with a class and type of algorithm.

- **Select the problem:** Select a problem or a set of questions you can use to test and validate the implementation of the algorithm.

- **Research about the algorithm:** Locate books, websites, libraries, and more to read and learn about the algorithm. There is a need to have one keystone description of the algorithm. This becomes useful because the multiple perspectives will help you to start the algorithm description faster and overcome roadblocks arising from ambiguities or assumptions.

5. **Evaluate the results:** Although essential, the follow-up phase is often neglected. During this phase, everything is arranged for successful completion of the project. Examples of activities in the follow-up phase include providing instructions and training for users, maintaining the result, and evaluating the project. The central question in this phase is when and where the project ends. The limits of the project should be considered at the beginning of a project so that it can be closed in the follow-up phase once it has reached those boundaries. Suppose, the project eventually produces excellent results. The team delivers a piece of software that works well in the testing phase, but when it is installed on the computers at a destination place, the prototype begins to have problems, and it sometimes gets unstable. For this reason, programmers should be able to repair the software.

Design and development knowledge representation

So far, we have discussed general problem-solving methodologies; now let's look at knowledge representation and reasoning, which are essential aspects of any artificial intelligence system and any computer system in general. In this section, we will discuss the classical methods of knowledge representation and reasoning in AI:

- **Knowledge representation and reasoning:** Artificial intelligence is a system that deals with the study of understanding, designing, and knowledge representation to computers. In any intelligent system, the description of knowledge is assumed to be an essential technique to encode that knowledge. The primary objective of an AI system is to design programs that can provide information to computers that can be helpful for interaction with humans and which can solve problems in various fields that require human intelligence.

- **The AI cycle:** In general, all AI systems have the following five components:

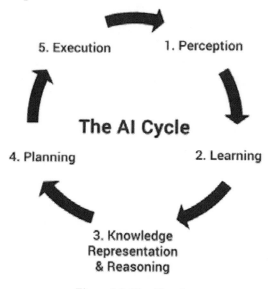

Figure 3.2: The AI cycle

The AI cycle shows the relationship between these components. The perception component of the AI system allows the system to collect information from the environment. With human perception, this may be audio, visual, or any other form of sensory information. The system must internally form a meaningful and useful representation of this collected information. This knowledge representation can be static, or it may collaborate with a learning component that is adaptive and predict trends from the perceived data.

Knowledge representation (KR) and reasoning are coupled with each other. Any description of knowledge is not meaningful on its own; it must be useful and helpful in achieving specific tasks. The same information can be represented in many different ways depending on how users want to use that information.

For example, in mathematics, if we're going to solve problems about statistics, we would most likely use regression models; but we can use other models too. Both can generate the same results, but the former model may be more suitable in scenarios where the user wants to perform reasoning on the information. So, it is essential at this point to understand how knowledge representation and reasoning are interdependent components; as an AI system developer, one has to consider this relationship when dealing with any solution.

In other words, we can say that knowledge is information about a particular domain that can be used to solve problems. Solving many problems requires knowledge in detail, and this knowledge must be represented in some manner. While designing an algorithm to solve problems, we must define the rules that show how the instructions will be represented. A representation specifies the form of knowledge. In general, there is a need to consider a set of rules that represent knowledge about relationships in the world and learn to solve the problem using the content of the rules.

Types of knowledge

Knowledge is a practical or theoretical understanding of a domain. In general, knowledge is more than just data; it consists of facts, beliefs, heuristics, ideas, rules, associations, abstractions, and relationships. The types of knowledge are explained below:

- **Procedural knowledge:** Procedural knowledge is a representation in which the control information that is necessary to use the knowledge is enclosed in the knowledge itself, such as computer programs.

  For example, consider the following:

  ```
  Woman (Engineer)
  Woman (Software Engineer)
  Company (XenonStack)
  ∀ x: Woman(x) → Company(x)
  ```

  The knowledge base justifies any of the following answers:

  ```
  Y=Engineer
  Y=Software Engineer
  Y=XenonStack
  ```

  We get more than one value that satisfies the predicate. If only one value is needed then the answer will depend on the order in which the assertions are observed during the search for a response.

- **Declarative knowledge:** This is a statement in which knowledge is specified but the method of using that knowledge is not given, for example, people's names, colors, and so on. These are facts that can stand alone and are not dependent on any other knowledge. So to use declarative representation, there is a need to have such a program that explains what to do with the knowledge and how to use that knowledge. Declarative learning refers to acquiring information that one can declare. For example, the population density of a particular place is a declarative piece of information.

- **Meta-knowledge:** Every domain such as computers, mathematics, science, or engineering is constituted as a knowledge object. The field that generates knowledge is particularly important for learning. The experience of a domain is called *meta-knowledge*. In other words, we can say that meta-knowledge is knowledge about knowledge, for example, the knowledge that blood pressure, pulse rate, or hemoglobin level is more important to diagnose a medical condition than eye color or height, and so on.

- **Heuristic knowledge:** Heuristic knowledge depends on the rule of thumb. It generates information based on a rule of thumb, which is helpful in guiding the reasoning process. In this type, knowledge is represented on essential strategies to solve problems through the experience of past problems by an expert. However, it is also known as shallow knowledge.

- **Structural knowledge:** Structural knowledge is the information that is based on a description of structures and their relationships such as rules, sets, concepts, and relationships. It provides the information necessary to develop the knowledge structures and the overall model of the problem. For example, think of the way various parts of an airplane fit together to make the airplane, or knowledge of structures with regards to concepts, subconcepts, and objects.

Representation

Multiple approaches and schemes come to mind when we begin to think about representation:

- **Pictures and symbols:** Pictures and symbols are the earliest way humans represented knowledge when sophisticated linguistic systems had not yet evolved. Every type of representation has its advantages. Various types of knowledge can be best described using pictures; for example, we can easily represent the relationship between employees in a company using an image. Also, we can use a series of images to store procedural knowledge. As we can see, pictures are suitable for recognition of tasks and representation of structural information. However, pictorial representations are not useful in transmitting information to computers because computers cannot interpret pictures directly without complex reasoning.

- **Graphs and networks:** Graphs and networks help to find relationships between objects/entities to be incorporated; for example, we can use a graph to show employee relationships.

- **Numbers:** Numbers are an essential part of knowledge representation used by humans. One can easily translate numbers into computer representations.

- **Knowledge representation:** This is an area of AI that aims at the representation of knowledge by using symbols to facilitate inference from those knowledge elements, creating new features of knowledge. Knowledge progression shows how data is moved through many phases, as shown here:

Knowledge Progression

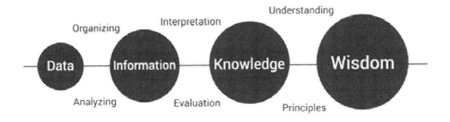

Figure 3.3: Representation of knowledge progression

The different phases of knowledge progression are explained below:

- Data is the collection of disconnected facts, for example, it is raining.

- Information appears when relationships between facts are established and understood, such as who, what, where, and when. For example, when the temperature dropped to 16 degrees, it started raining.

- Knowledge appears when relationships between patterns are identified and understood, such as how. For example, if the humidity increases and the temperature drops, the atmosphere is unlikely to hold on to moisture, thereby increasing the possibility of rains.

- Wisdom is the peak of understanding. It uncovers the principles of relationships that describe patterns such as why. For example, it encloses the understanding of all the interactions that happen between rain, air currents, evaporation, temperature gradients, changes, and raining.

Knowledge engineering

Knowledge engineering is the process of designing an **expert system (ES)**. It consists of three stages:

- **Knowledge acquisition:** The process of collection, elicitation, analysis, modeling, and validation of knowledge from experts through interviews and observations by human experts.

- **Knowledge representation:** Selecting the most applicable structures to represent knowledge such as lists, sets, object-attribute, value triplets, scripts, decision trees, and so on.

- **Knowledge validation:** Testing that the knowledge of the ES is correct and complete.

Expert system designers can use different elements to represent different kinds of knowledge. Knowledge representation elements could be primitives like rules, frames, semantic networks and concept maps, ontology, and logic expressions. These primitives may combine into more complex knowledge elements.

Whatever elements they use, experts must structure the knowledge so that the system can efficiently process it and humans can easily identify the results.

Representation techniques

For permitting the development of large and technical knowledge bases, representation of languages should have a single focus that facilitates knowledge evolution in exploration and validation. In this section, we will discuss various knowledge representation techniques.

Let us understand the various representations of knowledge one by one.

Knowledge representation using predicate logic

Predicate logic is a programming language with rules for syntax and semantics. The syntax consists of well-formed formulas that include logical symbols, predicate and function symbols, term, method, and sentence. Semantics means the meaning of a name or equation, that is, a set of elements. The meaning of a phrase is a truth value. The function that maps a formula into a set of components is called an *interpretation*. An interpretation maps an intentional description into an extensional description.

First-order logic extends propositional logic in two directions:

- It provides an inner structure for sentences that are viewed as relations between objects or individuals.
- It provides a means to express and reason with generalizations.

In predicate logic, there are three additional notations:

- **Terms:** First-order logic is used to represent objects or individuals. Terms can bea constant for a specific object, such as A, B, C, John, Blue, Green, and so on; variable for an unspecified object, such as x, y, z, and so on.; and functions for a specific object related in a certain way to other objects, such as Mother Of, Size Of, or color.
- **Predicates:** Predicates define a relation that binds two elements to have a value of true or false. A predicate can take arguments, known as terms.
  - o A predicate with one argument expresses a property of an object, for example, a company (Xenon).
  - o A predicate with two or more arguments indicates a relation between the objects for example likes (John, Navdeep).
  - o A predicate with void arguments is simple proposition logic.
- **Universal Quantifier:** A Universal Quantifier is used to identify the scope of a variable in a logical expression. For example, *Universal Quantifier of* $\forall x\ (Q(x))$ means for all x, Q of

x is true. For example, ∀ *x (intelligent(x))* if the universe is of people then this means that everyone is intelligent.

- **Existential Quantifier:** The statement Existential Quantifier of ∀ *x (Q(x))*, means there exists at least one x for which Q of x is true. For example, ∀ *x (Intelligent(x))*, if the universe is of people than this means there is at least one intelligent person.

Knowledge representation using semantic net

The semantic network is an alternative to predicate logic in the form of knowledge representation. The knowledge can be stored in the form of a graph, with nodes representing objects and arcs representing relationships between those objects. The semantic network is also known as *associative network*.

The semantic representation consists of 4 parts:

- **Lexical:** Lexical element represents symbols that are allowed in the description of vocabulary, like, nodes denote objects; links denote the relation between objects, and link-labels denote particular relations.

- **Structural:** It describes constraints on how the symbols can be arranged, for example, the way by which different nodes are connected to each other by links.

- **Procedural:** It specifies the access procedures, such as to create, modify, and answer questions. The types of procedures are constructor procedure, reader procedure, writer procedure, and erasure procedure.

- **Semantic:** It builds the way of associating the meaning. For example, nodes and links denote application specific entities.

Let's discuss the concept of semantic networks in AI by using the stored entities of the network objects and their relationships:

- They need to represent English sentences.
- Edges will be annotated with descriptors or relations.

Here is a semantic network widely used to represent sentences, for example:

- A canary can sing/fly.
- A canary is a bird/animal.

- A canary is a canary.
- A canary TEMP has skin.

The following diagram illustrates the semantic network:

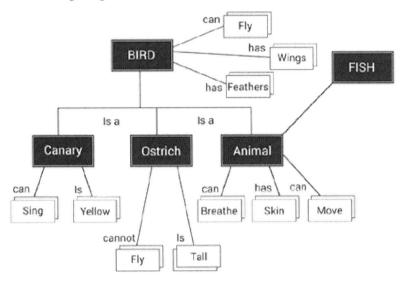

Figure 3.4: *Example of semantic networks*

Semantic network has the following properties as shown in *Figure 3.4*:

- **Is a:** It is a class/subclass.
- **Instance:** The first object is a class instance.
- **Has:** It contains or has a physical property.
- **Can:** It has the ability to do something.
- made of, color, texture, and so on

Knowledge representation using frames

A frame is a node with the structure that facilitates the differentiation of the relationships between objects and properties of objects. Sometimes it is also called as slot-and-filler representation. Frames are the application of object-oriented programming for expert systems.

Frames overcome the constraints of the semantic network that differentiates the relationships and properties of objects. Each frame represents a class or an instance. The concept of a structure is represented by a collection of slots. Each slot describes an appropriate attribute or operation of the frame. Slots are also used to store values.

A slot may contain a default value or a pointer to another frame, a set of rules or procedures by which the slot value is obtained.

A script is a precedent that consists of tightly coupled expecting-suggesting first action and state change frames. It is a structured representation describing a sequence of events in a particular context.

Knowledge representation using scripts

Scripts are useful in the prediction of unobserved events. As compared to scripts, a frame has relatively more knowledge about a particular object, location, activity, situation or another element. A frame can describe the object in great detail. The script, on the other hand, is a knowledge representation of the schemas that describe a sequence of events instead of defining an object.

Scripts are used for the following purposes:

- Interpret, understand, and reason about scenes.
- Understand and reason about events.
- Reason about actions.
- Plan actions to complete tasks.

A script is composed of scenes, props, actors, events, and acts. In each scene, one or more actors can perform actions. The actors act along with the props. The script represents a tree or network of states, driven by events.

As with frames, scripts drive interpretation by suggesting the system what to look for and where to look at. A script can predict events.

Let us take an example of a hotel script in which we define various features like scene, actors, props, acts:

- **Scene:** A hotel with an entrance, reception, tables, and chairs.
- **Actors:** The diners, chefs, and servers.
- **Props:** The table setting, menu, tables, and chairs.
- **Acts:** Entry, seating on the chair, ordering a meal, serving, eating, requesting the bill, paying, and leaving.

Knowledge representation issues

There are various issues to be considered regarding knowledge representation. Some of them are grain size - resolution detail, scope, modularity, understandability, explicit vs. implicit knowledge, and procedural vs. declarative knowledge. Let us understand some issues and their aspects.

Mathematical formulations of representing knowledge

Mathematical modeling is the task of translating problems from an application area into mathematical formulations whose theoretical and numerical analysis can provide answers, insights, and guidance to the new application. It is essential in many applications as it gives direction to solve a problem, enables a detailed understanding of the system model, helps in better design or control of a system, and allows the efficient use of modern computing capabilities.

Mathematical modeling is the activity concerning the study of the simulation of physical development by computational processes. The simulation aims to predict the behavior of an artifact within its environment. The following sections describe the applications and future impacts of AI technology on several mathematical modeling activities. The various mathematical modeling activities include generation of a model, interpretation of accurate results, development, and control of the numerical algorithms.

Here are the various algorithms that are used to extract numerical information from mathematical models:

- **Numerical linear algebra:**
  - o Eigenvalue problems
  - o Linear systems of equations
  - o Techniques for massive, sparse issues
  - o Linear programming (linear optimization)

- **Numerical analysis:**
  - o Function evaluation
  - o Special functions
  - o Interpolation
  - o Automatic and numerical differentiation
  - o Techniques for large, sparse problems
  - o Approximation (least squares, radial basis functions)

- o Integration (univariate, multivariate, Fourier transform)
- o Optimization = nonlinear programming
- o Nonlinear systems of equations

- **Numerical data analysis (numerical statistics):**
  - o Classification
  - o Prediction
  - o Visualization (2D and 3D computational geometry)
  - o Parameter estimation (least squares, maximum likelihood)
  - o Time series analysis (filtering, time correlations, signal processing, and spectral analysis)
  - o Random numbers and Monte Carlo methods
  - o Categorical time series (hidden Markov models)
  - o Techniques for large, sparse problem

- **Numerical functional analysis:**
  - o Ordinary differential equations (initial value problems, boundary value problems, eigenvalue problems, and stability)
  - o Partial differential equations (finite differences, finite elements, boundary elements, mesh generation, and adaptive meshes)
  - o Techniques for large problems
  - o Integral equations (and regularization)
  - o Stochastic differential equations
- Non-numerical algorithms:
- Symbolic methods (computer algebra)
- Cryptography
- Sorting
- Error correcting codes
- Compression

Model representation

By using the above algorithms, we can make a model in such a form that is accessible to the computer. The detailed modeling cycle is shown below:

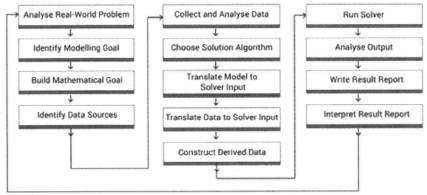

Figure 3.5: *Steps of modeling cycle*

To solve a problem, there is a need to analyze the real world and identify or say, find a goal. Further, we need to start building a suitable mathematical model according to the problem. Then, we need to collect data from various data sources, build a model, analyze output, and finally, make a detailed report interpreting the results.

Let's consider the problem of prediction of the election system. In this, various steps need to be followed to build a model successfully.

Analyze real-world problem

The goal is to build a 360 degree view of the product, brand, and celebrity through the data available on social media.

- **Identify modeling goal:** Develop a platform using ML, DL, and NLP for social media analytics and represent through data visualization tools like D3.js charts, Canvas.js, and more.

- **Build mathematical goals:** Principal component analysis, entropy, eigen decomposition, combinatorics, Gaussian, Bernoulli, Hessian, Jacobian, Laplacian, distributions, and Manifolds.

- **Identify data sources:** Facebook, Twitter, YouTube, LinkedIn, Instagram, news websites, Snapchat, and Pinterest.

- **Collect and analyze data:** The very first step of analytics is to bring the data into the system, that is, the data ingestion process. While ingesting data, we can have multiple data sources, therefore, we need a universal data ingestion platform where we can connect to various data sources and then process the data further. There is a need for a universal data ingestion platform because it makes it easy to monitor the ingestion process from various data sources. Various types of data analysis can be helpful, such as audience profile analysis, content analysis, competitive benchmarking, sentiment analysis, traffic analysis, community detection, fake news recognition, territory, and area mapping.

- **Choose solution algorithm:** Extra Trees Classifier, Gradient Boosting Classifier, Random Forest Classifier, Logistic Regression, Bernoulli NB, Gaussian NB, Multinomial NB, K Neighbors Classifier, Linear SVC, Nu SVC, SVC, Decision Tree Classifier, Naive Bayes Maximum Entropy Model, Autoencoders.

- **Translate model to solver input:** Train the model by taking historical data.

- **Translate data to solve input:** Pre-processing the data means to convert the data in a meaningful form. Clean and transform the data.

- **Construct derived data:** Extract the meaningful data or say, important features of the data that are helpful to predict the accurate results.

- **Run solver:** Build and run a model.

- **Analyze output:** Save the model and make daily predictions on the data and analyze the data. To do this we can use different types of charts like heatmap, line charts, bar charts, histograms, pie charts, and so on, based on our data and the requirements.

- **Write the result report:** After getting accurate results, the next step is to write a result report of the model in detail as along with the various phases used during model building.

- **Interpret result report:** Last but not the least step is to do a detailed interpretation of the report.

Strategies for searching possible solutions from the problem spaces

The ability to solve complicated scientific problems is considered one of the critical competencies customers should acquire. There are various approaches to model scientific problem solving, its structure, and its implementation. The strategies which are involved in scientific problem solving are different for different problems.

A successful scientist must master two related skills— knowing where to look and understanding what is seen. The first skill is the experimental design which involves the design of innovative and observational procedures. The second skill is hypothesis formation which involves the formation and evaluation of the theory.

There are two essential characterizations of the process of scientific reasoning. These are concept-formation view and problem-solving view. In the concept-formation view, scientific reasoning consists of forming new concepts by experimental evidence. Whereas in the problem-solving view, scientific reasoning is characterized as a search process.

Solution strategy

Suppose we have a problem in a particular domain, an expert might have different solution strategies. Intuitively, a solution strategy is available which means it can be used to deal with frequently occurring problem situations. For instance, in the domain of travel planning, the task could be of finding a route between two places. Let's take an example of Uber; depending on the available means of transportation, different strategies can be applied, for example, driving by taxi, taking an auto, or taking a shared cab.

In general, a solution strategy forms the basis of the process to find a solution. It might be complicated to hypothesize the solution strategy even if the solution itself contains too little information about the solution process. However, it might be challenging to hypothesize the solution strategy from the solution. The choice of the solution strategy is an important design decision for creating a solution. The general problems are classified into five classes according to an increasing size of the solution space:

- **Class 1 - One solution strategy and one implementation:** Problems of this type can be solved according to a single solution strategy and have only one solution. In some cases, the description of the issues of this class can be specified in such a way that the answer is unique. These kinds of problems are suited to recall elemental knowledge of the domain because the single solution can be used to address a concept that should be learned.

- **Class 2 - One solution strategy, alternative implementation variants:** This type of problems can be solved according to a single solution strategy which, however, can be implemented in many different ways. Issues at this level are precisely specified so that the space of possible solutions is narrowed down to a single solution strategy.

- **Class 3 - Limited number of alternative solution strategies:** In this class of problems, the customer is free to choose one of the several non-alternative solution strategies and they implement it according to their preferences. This class of problems is more challenging than Class 2 and Class 3 because developers have to make appropriate design decisions, that is, choosing between solution strategies and implementation variants, instead of merely applying a pre-defined solution template.

- **Class 4:** In this class, we have a significant variability of possible solution strategies; however, the correctness of any given specific solution can be verified. In this class, the problem is so complex that it needs to be solved by dividing it into sub-problems that can be solved using different solution strategies. Since the combination of solution strategies results in a new solution strategy for the overall task, the number of these combinations is not known as a priori.

- **Class 5:** In this class, we have a great variety of possible solution strategies and the correctness of solutions cannot be verified. Problems of this class require solutions that not only fulfill specific testable functional requirements but also the ones that should be considered useful and acceptable by a large number of stakeholders.

Let's take an example, the Uber taxi service was officially launched in 2010. Six months later, they had approximately 6,000 users and had already provided about 20,000 rides.

Uber works as a location-based startup from day one. To create the model of Uber, manufacturers need to understand the specifics of iOS and Android geolocation features. Let us go through the important features that should be considered:

- **Identifying a device's location:** The Uber app that works on iOS system uses the Core-Location framework to find a user's device. The Core-Location framework provides protocols to configure and schedule the location delivery and send back location events to the server. The Core-Location framework also helps Uber to define geographic locations and monitor a device's movements as it crosses the boundaries. For Android version of the Uber app, geolocation was implemented using Google's Location APIs that can manage location technology and meet various other development needs when implementing location-based features.

- **Providing driving directions to the driver:** To display point-to-point directions on a map, developers of the Uber app used MapKit for the iOS version. Registering the app as a routing application makes routes available to the Maps application and all other mapping software on a user's device. In Android, routes and directions are made possible by the Google Maps Android API.

- **Integrating Wi-Fi mapping software:** As Google Map is integrated with Uber; it helps Uber find the location for both iPhone and Android versions of their application. But Google Maps is not the only service that Uber uses. To avoid paying Google for access to their solutions, Uber buys mapping technology companies to solve their logistics issues.

- **Push notifications and SMS:** The user can receive these messages as SMS or push notifications. After a client books a ride, Uber sends some notifications such as:
    - o when a driver accepts your request
    - o when the driver is about to reach its destination
    - o when a ride has been canceled due to some reason

- **Payment integration:** Uber prefer to make their system cashless. The user can pay cash, pay via debit or credit card, or use a promo code; these modes of payment remove any human-to-human transactions. When accepting card payments, there are specific requirements that companies must comply with. Uber can also use PayPal's Cardio service for the scanning of credit cards on iOS. In Android, users need to manually enter credit card data to link a card to their Uber account.

- **Transportation with DL and AI at Uber:** Recently, Uber has started using **machine learning (ML), artificial intelligence (AI),** and advanced technologies to create positive experiences for users. They introduced a Bayesian neural network architecture that can estimate trip growth more accurately.

Among other areas, they use ML to enable an efficient ride-sharing marketplace, identify suspicious accounts, and suggest optimal pickup and drop off points.

- **Problem space:** Uber's problem is new and rapidly evolving, especially at the scale and intersection of dimensions:

  o **Temporal:** From seconds to years.

  o **Spatial:** At both micro levels (riders, cars, and goods) and macro levels (global, regional, and city).

  o **Active:** Immediate impact and response to the system.

  o **Human:** Involved at every stage, starting from decision making to decision receipt.

  o **Scale:** Millions of calculations and thousands of decisions made for riders and drivers every minute.

Designing Uber maps

Maps represent the physical world that is built on data, and Uber's primary mission is too tied to the ability to use this data to refine the mapping technologies. Aspects such as prediction and destination search, ETAs, generation of map tiles, routing, and fare estimates, maps are essential in every element of a logistics network. They can be represented visually by maps that cover more than 95 percent of pixels on the rider.

Uber uses ML to improve their maps. Destination prediction fulfills problems of all destination entries and tests the accuracy of models:

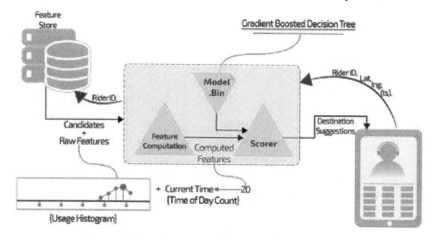

Figure 3.6: Flow of designing Uber maps

The destination prediction process consists of five distinct steps:

1. Rider books taxi to ride.

2. The service retrieves details of the rider from the stored feature and ranks them by providing latitude, longitude and time.

3. The system service returns the first seven destination suggestions along with selected candidates from places where people have previously traveled and searched.

4. By using a combination of information about the physical world along with ML, the service produces a list of places along with the set of features, including a histogram of popular destinations with corresponding request times and the current time.

5. A machine-learned scorer then ranks these suggested places, taking feedback from another model that learned to train how to weight all the components separately.

Uber service architecture

In the marketplace, some models describe the world and the decision engines that act on the models. The following diagram illustrates the architecture of Uber service:

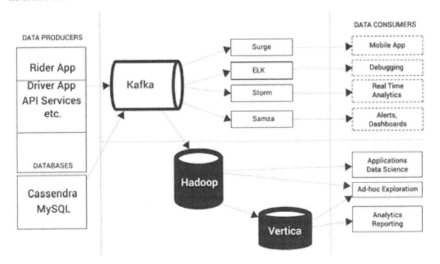

Figure 3.7: Architecture diagram of Uber service

This architecture diagram shows the working of Uber. On the left-hand side, it's mostly where the data comes from, that is, all the applications, services, and databases. They all go into one central piece, which is Kafka. From here, many services pull the data through consumers. Surge pulls data to do some fair calculations.

ELK (Elasticsearch, Logstash, and Kibana) is the logging stack. It is used to provide real-time reporting dashboards used for debugging, reporting, and auditing. Samza and Flink pull data to do real-time data processing. The same data is sent to S3 for cold storage, where it can be kept for archives. The same Kafka has Hadoop as a consumer. Once information is stored in Hadoop, it can be used for batch processing, ad hoc queries, and data exploration. Hadoop's data repository is used to run data science applications.

Conclusion

After this tour around decision making and human reasoning, we can draw some conclusions. The first is that decision theory and AI are only at the beginning of their mutual cross-fertilization. The decision theory is all about making the best decision, either in a particular or uncertain world with the available choices. AI has focused much attention on diagnosis and human knowledge representing and recording. It is only a few years following its first embraced uncertainty and has practically never dealt with decisions. For some reason, the planning process starts after the decision is made since the result of the decision is the goal. It is indeed possible to ignore the preferences and to help a user find the right path from the current state to their goal, but AI cannot carry out that plan without paying attention to uncertainty. So, AI and decision theory appear to be mainly complementary— diagnosis representation and handling of the recorded states for AI, look-ahead, uncertainty, and preferences for decision theory.

Questions

1. What are the main steps to solve a problem? Describe each of them briefly.

2. Describe different types of knowledge.

3. What is AI cycle? What are the main steps involved in it? Describe each step briefly.

4. What are the different steps involved in the development cycle of a model? Describe each step briefly.

CHAPTER 4

Intelligent Computing Strategies by Google

In this chapter, we will learn about the progress of deep learning by Google Inc. This chapter includes the achievements of intelligent services currently provided by the company and recent exploration by DeepMind, a subsidiary of Google that is working hard on achieving new frontiers in DL research. We'll also discuss the business model of the company revolving around the use of deep learning technologies.

Structure

- The strategies of Google Inc. in in-depth learning exploration
- Research environment by DeepMind and other services provided to the users
- Business models currently adopted by the company
- How Google is going to impact the current businesses

Objective

Understanding of current progresses on deep learning research by Google and DeepMind to provide better services.

The strategies of Google in deep learning exploration

In the last few years, AI and DL were applied to solve hundreds of problems, from computer vision to natural language processing. In all cases, DL defeats previous work. DL is widely used in both, academics to study intelligence and in the industry to build intelligent systems that can assist humans in various tasks.

The goal of this chapter is to share essential applications of deep learning that can be used by Google in the field of text, search, voice, and computer vision.

One of the essential areas of DL application is working with the text—translation, text analysis, chatbots, and a plethora of other tasks.

- **Google Neural Machine Translation (GNMT):** Google's machine translation could make it easier for people to communicate with those speaking a different language, by translating speech directly into text in a language they can understand. Machine translation of speech works typically by first converting it into text, then translating that text into the desired language. Thus, any error in speech recognition will lead to incorrect transcription and consequently, incorrect translation.

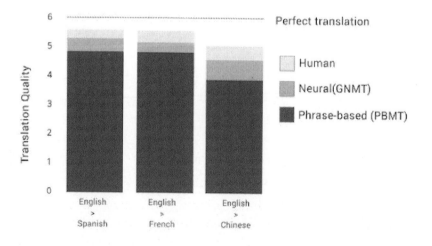

Figure 4.1: Comparison of the translation quality of human, neural-based model, and phrase-based model

The team trained its system on hundreds of hours of English audio with corresponding Spanish, French, and Chinese text. In each case, it uses severallayers of neural networks (computer systems loosely modeled on the human brain) to match sentences of spoken French with the written translation.

- **Chatbot:** Google has been moving towards the chatbot space. Google Assistant can suggest movies or restaurants directly within a conversation taking place at Allo. Google further improved with the recent launch of the latest tool named Chatbase. It is an analytical tool that helps companies develops their chatbots that are used in several social media tools like Facebook Messenger. It helps these companies improve their chatbots; it also allows Google to get relevant information about the other field. The idea behind Chatbase cloud service is to offer tools to analyze and optimize chatbots more efficiently. These tools enable bot builders to create features that help increase customer conversions and improve the bot's accuracy, thereby creating a better user experience.

- **Speech processing and generation:** Another relevant field of DL application used by Google is speech processing. It includes the production of speech and music, recognition and synchronization of the lip movements, and so on. Nowadays, **Automatic Speech Recognition (ASR)** is used in daily real-life applications. One of the primary goals of speech recognition is to allow communication between humans and computers via speech in the ways humans interact with each other.

Google's first attempt at speech recognition driven directory assistance service, which worked from any phone, came in 2007 and was called GOOG-441. It was a speech-enabled business finder that took user's spoken words (city, state, business name, and business address) as input. Based on the relevance between the match and the query, one to eight results were read back to the user using **text-to-speech (TTS).** The user then had the option to get connected to the service or request an SMS with the business information.

Google's current speech recognition system is speaker-independent and is built using deep neural networks, together with hidden Markov models (DNN-HMM). The strength of Google Speech helps in general-purpose tasks like making search requests on the **World Wide Web (WWW).** Google uses cloud-computing for speech recognition tasks.

- **Google Maps for Mobile (GMM):** In March 2008, Google introduced multimodal speech applications for GMM. GMM can show the location of a business and other related information directly on a map. The contact information, address, and any additional meta-information about a company (such as ratings) can readily be displayed. Also, due to the multi-modality of the search experience, the total time spent is significantly less. Finally, the cognitive load on the user is reduced. These advantages enable substantial improvement in the quality of interaction and quality of information.

- **Google Search by Voice:** In November 2008, Google launched Voice Search that works on various types of smartphones. Voice Search merely adds the ability to speak to the phone and ask a query instead of typing into the browser. The audio message is sent to Google servers where it is recognized and the result is sent back to the mobile. The data moves over the data channel instead of the voice channel, which provides higher quality audio transmission and better recognition rates. **Google Mobile App (GMA)** for the iPhone included a search by voice feature. GMA search by voice extended the paradigm of multi-modal voice search from searching for businesses on maps to exploring the entire WWW.

- **DeepMind WaveNet:** Google DeepMind is developing WaveNet — an algorithm that can transform the input text into raw audio. It can show outstanding results as compared to previous attempts. It is one of the fully convolutional neural networks where it contains various dilation factors that allow its respective corresponding field to grow exponentially with depth and cover thousands of steps. At the time of training, input sequences are original waveforms obtained by recording human speakers. After training, the sampling of data is used to generate synthetic utterances. During the sampling process, the value is extracted from the probability distribution computed by the network. After that, the obtained value is fed back into the input and a process of new prediction is done.

- **Lip reading from Google DeepMind:** Google DeepMind is an artificial intelligence analysis within Google. DeepMind is inspired by neuroscience that helps to make progress in many areas such as reasoning, imagination, learning, and memory. Taking vision, for example, human ability plays an essential part in our daily lives; it allows us to plan and to reason about the future, but it is very challenging for computers. Keeping this in mind, imagination augmented agent was introduced which can extract relevant information from an environment to plan what to do in the future.

  These are systems that learn automatically. They're not pre-programmed and not even handcrafted features. Google provides a broad set of raw information to the algorithms so that the systems themselves can learn the very best representations and use those for action, classification, or predictions. The reinforcement learning architecture is mostly a design approach to develop systems that begin with an agent. The agent has a policy that governs its interaction with an environment. This environment could be a trading environment, a small physics domain, or it could be a real-world robotics environment. The agent says that it wants to take action in this environment and gets feedback for the situation in the form of observations. Further, it uses these observations to update its policy of behavior or its model of the world.

- **Synchronization of the lip movement with the audio stream:** Lip reading is the impressive ability to recognize words and phrases from visual information alone. Lip-reading is difficult for a novice. Many deaf people can do it, but it is challenging. Human lip reading performance is quite average. Hearing-impaired people achieve an accuracy of only 17±12%. An important goal, therefore, is to automate lip reading. Machine lip reading is difficult because it requires extracting spatiotemporal features from the video. With AI like Google's DeepMind, it is now possible to analyze lip movement in visuals and do a better job than humans. Google made an algorithm with DeepMind, which is able to read lip movement of humans, as shown in the following diagram:

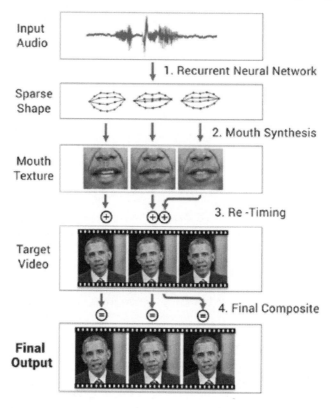

Figure 4.2: Transformation of the data with respect to each step

The neural network system first converts the input in the form of audio (sound) to time-varying mouth shape. Based on this mouth shape, photo-realistic mouth texture is generated, which is further composited into the mouth region of an existing target video and speech.

Research environment by DeepMind and other services provided to the users

AI research has made considerable progress in a variety of domains ranging from speech recognition, image classification, and genomics to drug discovery. In many cases, there are specialist systems that gain enormous amounts of human expertise and data. Let's get an overview of some of the AI services in various fields.

AlphaGo

AlphaGo was the first program needed to achieve superhuman performance in Go. It utilized two deep neural networks— a policy network that outputs move probabilities, and a value network that outputs a position evaluation. The policy network was initially trained by supervised learning to predict the moves of human experts accurately and then refined by policy-gradient reinforcement learning. The value network was trained to anticipate the winner of games played by the policy network against itself.

Once trained, further networks were combined with a *Monte-Carlo Tree Search*. This was done to provide a look-ahead search using the policy network to narrow down the search to high-probability moves and using the value network to evaluate positions in the tree. A convolutional neural network is used to approximate the policy network; the network structure is roughly something that follows, showing an example of a **Convolutional Neural Network (CNN):**

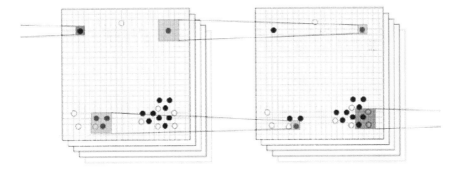

Figure 4.3: Network structure of ANN

The following points give a brief layer wise introduction of the Network:

- **Input:** 19 x 19 x 48 vector representing the state of a particular move.

- **Hidden layers:** various convolutional layers with various window sizes.

- **Output:** A softmax layer of size 19 x 19 x 2. The first 19 x 19 represent possible moves for the black player, and the other 19 x 19 output is for the white player.

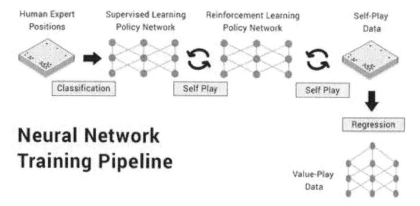

Figure 4.4: Training pipeline of Neural Network

- **Supervised learning of policy networks:** Supervised learning (SL) of policy network is a CNN of 13 layers that was trained on 30 million moves of human experts. The supervised learning policy network achieved 57.0% accuracy. Also, training a rollout policy on a corpus of 8 million movements attained an efficiency of 24.2%.

- **Reinforcement learning of policy networks:** While the SL policy network is excellent in predicting the next most likely moves, RL helps with the prediction of the best possible (winning) moves. The reinforcement learning policy aims to improve the SL policy through self-play. The reinforcement learning policy network had the same architecture. At this stage, AlphaGo played 1.2 million games with randomly selected previous iterations of itself. The goal of this policy was to adjust it towards the real purpose of winning games rather than maximizing predictive accuracy. Reinforcement learning can earn more than 80% of games as compared to SL policy.

The following diagram displays a comparison between value network and policy network:

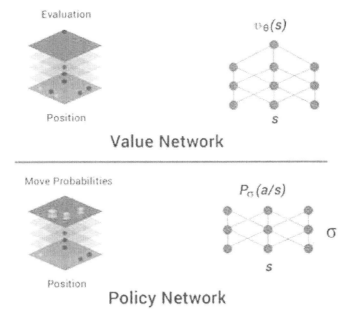

Figure 4.5: Comparison of value-based network and policy network

- **Reinforcement learning of value network:** The value network tries to predict, for a given position, which player has the advantage. Here is just a CNN trained with the least-squares regression method. During self-play, data comes from the board positions and outcomes. Policy and value networks search AlphaGo and use a combination of policy and value networks in the Monte Carlo search tree. The following diagram illustrates the four phases:

Figure 4.6: Flow of selection, expansion, evaluation, and backup

The game tree is searched in simulations composed of four phases:

- **Selection:** Simulation traverses tree by selecting edges with maximum action value Q.

- **Expansion:** If any node is expanded, it is processed once by the SL policy network to get prior probabilities for each legal action.

- **Evaluation:** Each node is evaluated by the value network and by FRpolicy.

- **Backup:** Values collected during the evaluation step updates action values Q.

  When time dedicated to a game agent is over, it chooses the best move based on the highest action value Q.

Autonomous cars

Self-driving cars are also known as driverless cars, autonomous cars, or robotic cars. Autonomous vehicles have already been developed and allowed on the roads. Currently, cars are semi-automated and require human control in some cases.

It is the first driverless electric car built by Google to test the next stage of its self-driving car project. It looks like a Smart car and a Nissan Micra with two seats and enough room space for a small amount of luggage.

Autonomous cars work with the use of various technologies which include GPS, laser light, radar, computer vision, and more. Many companies are investing in Self-driving cars as it may, one day, dominate the market. There are many challenges in the field of research; however, best researchers in the industry are involved in it. There is a legal framework that surrounds the fair-use of self-driving cars. Security concerns have also been raised for self-driving vehicles.

The car can carry two people from one place to another without any interaction with the user. A smartphone notifies the vehicle for pick up at the exact location of the user with the destination set. There is no manual control or steering wheel. It has merely a start button and an emergency stop button of red color. In front of the passengers, there is a screen that shows the current speed, the weather, and more.

Once the journey is over, the small screen displays a message to remind the user to take their personal belongings. Let's go through the car's hardware specifications:

- **Radar:** Traditional radars are used to detect dangerous objects in the path of the vehicles, which are more than 100 meters away. Systems trigger alerts when they sense something in the car's blind spot. The radar chirps between 10 and 11 GHz over five milliseconds, transmitting the radar signal from a centrally located antenna cone. Two receive cones, separated by 14 inches approximately, receive the reflected radar energy.

- **Optics:** A camera fixed near the rear-view mirror build real-time 3D images of the road ahead that can spot hazards like pedestrians and animals. It is also used to identify traffic signals and road markings.

- **Light Detection and Ranging (LIDAR):** LIDAR is an essential device in the autonomous vehicles that is placed on the roof of the car. It consists of an emitter, receiver, and mirror. The emitter sends a LASER beam that bounces off a mirror that rotates along with a cylindrical cover at ten revolutions per minute. After bouncing off objects, the LASER beam returns to the mirror and is bounced back towards the receiver where it can interpret it as data. The vehicle can then generate a map of its surroundings and use the map to avoid objects.

- **Global Positioning System (GPS):** A GPS keeps the car on its expected route, having an accuracy of 30 centimeters. With GPS that covers the macro location of the vehicle; on-deck cameras can recognize more minor details like red lights, stop signs, and construction zones.

- **Processors:** Processors with seven dual-core, 2.13 GHz, and 2 GB RAM configurations are needed to process the data collected by the car's instruments. Some vehicles can run as many as 17 processors to dispense the computing load.

- **Wheel Speed Sensors:** Wheel speed sensors measure the wheel speed and direction of rotation on the road. These sensors provide input to different automotive systems, which include the anti-lock brake system and electronic stability control.

Working of autonomous car

The autonomous car is mechanized by an electric motor with a range of around a 100-mile. It uses the software as well as a combination of sensors to locate itself in the real-world with the combination of highly accurate digital maps. In most cars, a GPS is used as the satellite navigation system to get a rough idea about the location of the vehicle, at which point lasers, radar, and cameras take over to monitor the 360-degree view of the world around the car. The following diagram shows the flow between the different parts of an autonomous car:

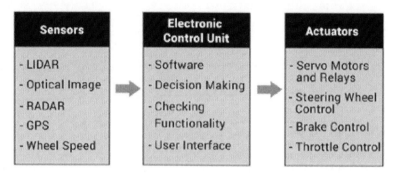

Figure 4.7: *Flow between the different parts of an autonomous car*

The software can quickly recognize objects, cars, people, road signs, and traffic lights, making the car obey the traffic rules and avoid several unpredictable hazards, including cyclists. For example, the Google autonomous car can successfully identify a cyclist and understand that if the cyclist extends an arm, they are expected to make a maneuver. The vehicle then knows to slow down and give the cyclist enough space to operate safely. It can even detect road works and safely navigate around them.

The software can recognize traffic signs and store them in a standard database using Google Maps and GPS. The GPS software component records the signs and direction of travel from that area. Every car operational in that area and using this software will register the new signs detected and modify the degree of confidence and degree of recognition for other users.

Another software component can recognize the separation lines between lanes. It uses three cameras to calculate precisely and to use probabilities about the position of the car on the road. From the location, the user can propose a new direction in the absence of traffic signs for the next few seconds.

Also, the software uses AI to detect other car fingerprints from Webcam images.

Google Play

Google launched Instant Apps Google Play Protect that provides a way for developers to give users an application in which there is no need to install anything. Users would click on a link on the search results page, and the instant app will load. Today, the companies are extending this program to games.

The features of the application are enabled by default on all Android devices that show that it is meant to be a real-time malware scanner that will scan every installed or about-to-be installed application and give information to the users in case of any suspicious activity.

DeepMind HealthStream application

A stream is a secure mobile phone application that aims to address the problems of patients when they are not able to get the necessary treatment at the right time. Thousands of people end up in hospitals due to preventable diseases like sepsis and acute kidney injury because they don't receive medical aid on time.

Google built streams to help doctors address this problem. The application brings together essential medical information, like patients' blood test results, in one place. If anyone is found sick, streams can send a secure and urgent smartphone alert to the right clinician to provide necessary help to the patient, along with information about their previous conditions so they can make an immediate diagnosis accordingly.

Streams can also allow clinicians to instantly review the vital signs of patients, like blood pressure, heart rate, as well as help to record these observations straight into the application. To make all of this possible, Streams integrates various types of data like lab data, medical data, text data, and test results from a range of existing IT systems used by the hospital.

AI navigation without a map

In today's digitally connected world, users are entirely dependent on Google Maps and other GPS elements that guide them to their destination. If we are familiar with a route or a place, we use our memories and visual cues to reach our destination. But what if there was no GPS and it was an entirely new place?

DeepMind's research team at Google has built an interactive navigation platform that makes use of first-person point-of-view pictures from Google Street View to train its AI model. The team developed a deep neural network artificial agent to continuously learn to navigate different cities using the visual information it gathers from images of Street View. Once it familiarizes itself with a few cities, it is able to adapt to a new city very quickly. Note that faces, images, and license plates are blurred and are unrecognizable in street-view, thereby ensuring privacy for people.

They built a neural network agent that takes inputs as images observed from the environment and predicts the next action it can make in that environment. They trained an end-to-end model using deep reinforcement learning.

The neural network inside an agent consists of three parts:

- **A convolutional network:** It can process images and extract visual features.

- **A locale-specific recurrent neural network data:** This involves memorizing the environment as well as learning a representation of the current position of the agent and location of the goal.

- **A locale-invariant recurrent network data:** It is designed to be interchangeable and unique to each city where the agent navigates.

Deep Q-Network (DQN)

DeepMind introduced the **Deep Q-Network (DQN)** algorithm in 2013. DeepMind created a system that learns to play video games by selecting actions based on only the screen images and the reward signal.

Supervised learning is not appropriate to interpret the higher dimensional sensor data. It is because the machine may have to learn without a supervisor telling it about the output of the possible input-output function. Therefore, reinforcement learning is introduced to determine the action in the current state to maximize an accumulated future reward. Before training, the program does not know anything about the game. It doesn't see the objective of the game, it has no understanding about its influence on the game, and it cannot even look at the objects in the game. By trial and error method, the system gradually learns to behave to receive a reward. The system uses the same architecture for different games without any game-related hints from the programmers other than the possible actions that are in the game, for example, up, down, left, right, space (fire), and so on.

Q-Learning is a reinforcement learning algorithm used for model-free optimal selection policy for a Markov chain process. But it is a classical approach and has one limitation. The limitation is that the number of possible states has to be reduced from infinity to the discrete states. Therefore, a technique was built with a combination of Q-Learning and deep neural networks. This technique is known as DQN. It can easily handle continuous inputs, so there is no need to have discrete data.

The following improvements are made to transform an ordinary Q-Network into DQN network:

- Moving from a single-layer network to multilayer convolutional neural networks.

- Implementation of experience-replay, which allows the network to train itself with the use of stored memories.

- A second target network is utilized to compute the target Q-values.

Working of DQN

The Bellman equation is used for training the DQN Network. Therefore, gradient descent and alpha as a loss are reduced from the equation. This obtained equation is set as a target to calculate the loss function. The model predicts the **Mean Squared Error (MSR)** between the Q-value.

Next, we need to train the neural network. Two feed-forward passes and one backpropagation pass is used for preparing the model. In the case of the feedforward pass, the state is taken as an input. The 1XN matrix highlighting the quality value of each action plan is obtained as an output.

Firstly, the state is passed to the neural network to determine the estimation of quality for each action. The action with the highest quality is selected using the Q-table and the respective work is performed. The next state is passed on to the neural network after observing it. For the computation of the target value, the most significant Q-value in the output is followed, and modified Bellman equation is used. After that, MSE is calculated between the first forward pass; it targets them and finally propagates it back through the neural network.

The following diagram illustrates the architecture of DQN:

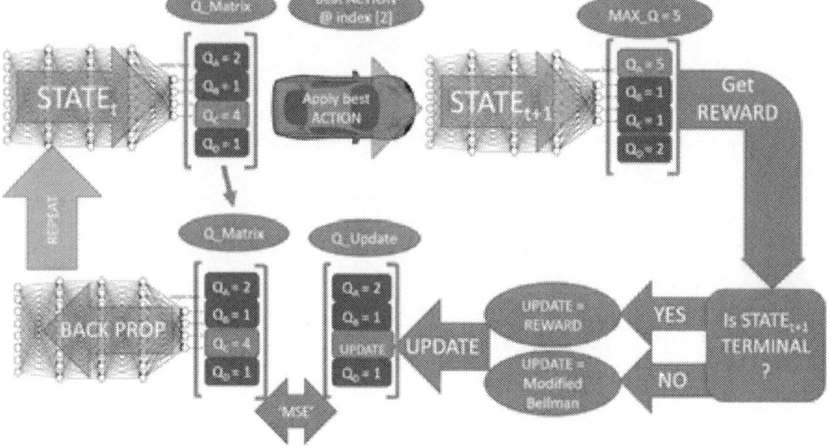

Figure 4.8: Architecture of DQN Network

DQN Network works by four techniques to overcome learning. The four techniques are experience replay, target network, clipping rewards, and skipping frames that are explained as follows:

- **Experience replay:** It is a technique to store previous experiences such as state, transitions, rewards, and actions that are highly important to perform Q-learning and build mini-batches to update the neural network.

- **Target network:** Due to the introduction of TD error computation, the target function keeps on changing with the Deep Neural Network. Therefore, the target network technique is used to fix the parameters of the target function, and after every thousand steps, the function is updated with the latest network.

- **Clipping rewards:** It is one of the DQN techniques used to clip the scores of the respective game so that all positive rewards are set as +1 and all negative rewards as -1.

- **Skipping frames:** For the reduction of the computational cost of ALE and to gather better experiences, the skipping frame technique is highly recommended. This technique of DQN is used to calculate the Q-values after every four frames and use the past four frames as an input for the neural network.

Business models currently adopted by Google

Business models are used to bridge the gap between strategy (the objectives, positioning, and goals of the company) and business processes (understanding and implementation of strategic information).

The business model canvas of Google explains the different aspects of a business model, such as customer segments, value propositions, channels, customer relations, revenue stream, key activities, cost structure, key partners, and key resources.

The Google business model can be better recognized if it is split into the following key areas:

- **Infrastructure**
  - o **Key activities:** Key activities consist of research and development for the development of new technologies along with the improvement of existing ones. Also, an exceptional amount of time spent in the maintenance and management of IT infrastructures, products, and services. There is also work done on marketing, strategy, and alliances.
  - o **Key partners:** Key partners for Google consist of distributors, suppliers, original equipment manufacturers, and the Open Handset Alliance.
  - o **Key resources:** Key resources for Google include data centers, servers, IPs, human support, and other IT infrastructure. Other resources include licenses, patents, and proprietary material.
- **Offering**
  - o **Value proposition:** Value proposition consists of offers of Google; the company creates value for its customers regarding internet search, advertising, operating systems, platforms, and enterprise.
- **Customers**
  - o **Customer segment:** Google customers are divided into three categories, which are as follows:
    - ▪ Users who organize information in convenient ways using Google products and services.

- Advertisers who have a cost-effective way to display online and offline ads to customers.
- Content providers who use the AdSense service.

o **Customer relationships:** Channels created to build customer relationships include sales and support services as well as dedicated team members for larger customers.

o **Channels:** Channels used to reach customers include Google affiliate websites, google.com, and Google AdWords. Channels are also used to reach advertisers and network members including sales and support teams.

- **Finances**

o **Cost structure:** Cost Structure for Google include the IT infrastructure, R&D costs, people, and marketing costs.

o **Revenue streams:** The primary revenue stream for the company includes its ad-powered search engine.

Google business model canvas

The Google business model canvas explains various aspects of customer segments, value proposition, channels, customer relationships, revenue streams, essential resources, key activities, partner network, and cost structure as shown in the following diagram:

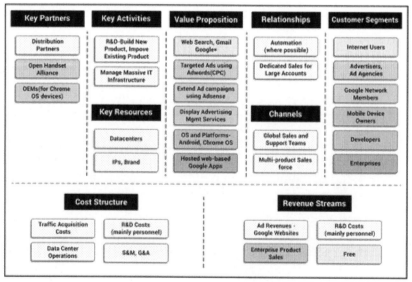

Figure 4.9: *Google Business Model Canvas*

Let us discuss the preceding figure by exploring all points one by one:

- **Key partners:** As Google has a multi-sided business platform; it forms key partners to bring new customers. It also uses these critical partnerships to retain old customers by offering new services. Without keeping those key partners, Google's revenue would drop vitally. Google earns 97% of its revenues from advertisements.

- **Key activities:** To operate successfully, Google has three principal activities that allow them to generate revenue and helps improve the value of offers for their customers.

  o Building and maintaining the search infrastructure.

  o Managing the three primary services. (AdWords, AdSense, and Google.com).

  o Promoting the platform to new users, content owners, and advertisers.

- **Network/platform:** Google continuously innovates new services and renovates its current search engine platform to make it better and faster.

- **Problem-solving:** Providing any service to a customer requires problem-solving. Each user using a Google service may interpret that service differently and varieties of new problems can arise. Google has the technology and human resources to eliminate any severe problems before they get out of control.

- **Key resources:** A vital resource is a fundamental requirement of every business model. With Google's essential resources, they can offer value propositions to their customers.

  o **Physical resources:** Key physical resources that Google has, includes 85 offices in over 40 countries. Their central office in California, known as the Googleplex, provides employees with substantial perks. In those offices, the technology equipment that they use to power their sites is of utmost importance.

  o **Intellectual:** Google's most prominent vital resources are its intellectual properties, which include design patents, hardware patents, medical patients, multiple database indexing, modeling and mapping patents, email, and messaging patents. It also includes radio patents, event modeling patents, social networking, search indexing patents, duplicate content patents, advertising patents, voting patents, image and video patents, game patents, and many more.

- **Value propositions:** Google developed a very user-friendly platform that is capable of establishing a connection between people and knowledge, which can be used to increase the efficiency in user experience. This ability became successful in attracting customers from a different bandwidth, who are ready to utilize Google's free service and also help to promote an advertising environment for business. This can provide advantages to both end-users as well as to enterprises.

  o **Google News:** Google News enables users to stay in touch with the different happenings all over the globe in a clear and organized manner with a categorization of subjects.

  o **Google Search:** Google provides the ability to use the state of the art search techniques with the latest technologies with high precision and accuracy.

  o **Google Finance:** The primary function of Google finance is to provide aid in the tracking of management and investment of a specific portfolio, acquire the knowledge on stock, and to gather all the latest news and information related to the trading market.

  o **Picasa:** Picasa is a platform under Google that is used to share videos and photos with family and friends.

  o **Google Talk:** Google talk lets you talk to your friends and family members. This tool is very advantageous as it is also gets connected to Gmail (Google Mail).

  o **Google Mail:** Google Mail is an email account service that is considered to be very secure. An email address is assigned to the user when he/she subscribes to Google, which can be used to stay in touch with anyone who is their contact. Another advantage is that it provides the ability to upload files and documents which is powered by online cloud device storage.

  o **Google Sites:** Google sites provide the ability to create free websites using multiple templates, and it is considered a user-friendly platform in which customization of the individual sections is possible. It is easy to add photos, services, and videos to integrate into the site, which can help generate revenue through the services of advertising.

o **Advertising value:** Google generates different incentives and benefits for different areas related to the businesses on the internet by using different varieties of services.

o **YouTube:** In 2006, YouTube was acquired by Google, and nowadays, it is the most used platform in terms of video surfing. YouTube completely changed the online video surfing space. Everyone can post videos and earn money through the advertising feature of YouTube.

o **AdWords:** This feature provides the ability to advertise something through the Google content network. These ads are displayed with the search results and also on YouTube when a user inputs a search query or surfs videos.

- **Customer relationships:** A company should clarify the customer and the type of relationship it wants to establish with the customer segment. The relationships between people and automation may vary. The following motivations can drive customer relationship:

    o Customer retention

    o Customer acquisition

Google has a close relationship with customers and advertisers. They create a virtual user community in which users are able to interact and exchange information or services. Google creates a user account that gives them many benefits like email, a social platform, calendars for organizing, and much more.

Channels to build customer relationships can include sales and support services, as well as dedicated teams for larger customers.

- **Sales and support:** Google believes that strong sales and support infrastructure is crucial to its success. They build relationships with the advertising world in a variety of ways such as direct, remote, and online sales channels. Technology and automation are used possibly to enhance the overall customer experience, ease of use, and cost-effectiveness.

- **Google accounts:** The creation of a user account on Google is free and has a lot of advantages for the end-user. Products offered with a Google account are free to use, such as Gmail, Google Maps, IGoogle, Google Chrome, and Google Sites. The use of these free tools allows users to build a relationship with Google.

- **Global Support organization:** In this, Google invests all of its efforts into helping Google network members and advertisers to get the benefit out of their tasks and work they are handling.

- **Channels:** On a global scale, the Google network reaches around 80% of internet users. Google reaches all across the industry from large well-known firms to smaller sites that are adapting according to the changes in the market.

- **Customer segment:** It defines the groups of people or organizations that it wants to reach and serve. Customers are the heart of any business model. Without customers, no company can survive for long. To satisfy the customer, a company may classify them into different segments with everyday needs, behaviors, or other conventional attributes. A business model may define several large or small customer segments. An organization needs to decide the part that has to be served and the portion that has to be ignored. Once the decision is made, a business model can be designed according to a keen understanding of specific customer needs.

The main customers of Google are the users who can organize information in useful ways using Google products and services, and the advertisers who have a cost-effective method to display online and offline advertisements to customers and Google Network Members.

- **Cost structure:** Primary costs for Google include traffic acquisition cost, IT infrastructure, data center operations, people, R&D costs, sales, and marketing costs.

- **Revenue streams:** Significant revenues of Google are generated from website advertising alone. Innovations like AdSense, AdWords, Google Mobile, and customers' relationship with Google also contribute. YouTube made Google a hugely successful advertising platform.

How Google will impact current businesses?

Google has provided different tools in the form of products and services that change the business world drastically. Google has offered many services such as Google search (fast communication, tracking, and captures the location in real-time), robotics, Google cars, artificial intelligence, smart messaging, weather information in real-time, and many more. (For some examples of Google products, see the following figure). These services and products are elements that will impact the current businesses. These elements are not only giving a new direction to modern-day innovation but also increasing the competition in the market, which will push other companies to perform better:

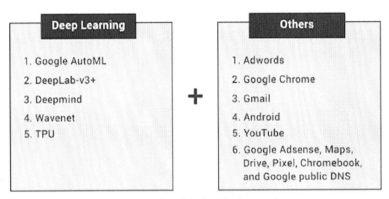

Figure 4.10: Google DL and other products

Google AutoML

AutoML Vision of Google is a new service that helps developers with limited machine learning expertise to build a custom image recognition model. Human-machine learning experts to perform the following tasks:

- Preprocessing and cleaning of the data.
- Selection and construction of appropriate features.
- Selection of an appropriate model family.
- Optimization of model hyperparameters.
- Post processing of machine learning models.

- Analyzing the obtained results.

The original idea of AutoML is to allow anybody to bring their images virtually, upload them, and then Google's systems automatically create a custom machine learning model for them. The whole process, from importing data to tagging and training the model, is done through a drag and drop interface.

With the use of AutoML, the accuracy of the model increases and results in faster turn around time:

- **Increased accuracy:** Cloud AutoML Vision is built on image recognition approaches that include machine learning and neural architecture technologies. This means AutoML helps to get a more accurate model.

- **Faster turnaround time:** With Cloud AutoML, the developer can create a model in minutes to sense AI-enabled application, or able to build the production-ready model in very less time.

- **Easy to use:** AutoML Vision provides a simple graphical user interface that helps to specify data and turns that data into a high-quality model customized according to the specific needs.

DeepLab-v3+

DeepLab-v3+ is Google's open-source Semantic Image Segmentation model. It is a deep learning model for semantic image segmentation to assign semantic labels (for example, cat, dog, person, and so on) to each pixel in the input image. The following figure is an illustrated view of the flow chart of DeepLab-v3+:

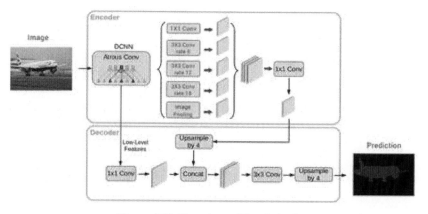

Figure 4.11: Flow chart of DeepLab-v3+

DeepLab-v3+ is implemented in TensorFlow and its models are built on the top of a convolutional neural network backbone architecture, which is intended for server-side deployment for the most accurate results. It is the extension of the DeepLab-v3 model. The DeepLab-v3 model consists of the convolution layer to extract the features by deep learning neural networks at an arbitrary resolution.

An estrous convolutional layer is a tool to control the features computed by deep learning models explicitly and to capture multi-scale information; it adjusts the filter field of view. It also generalizes the standard convolution operation.

For the development of the DeepLab-v3+ model, a simple and active decoder module is added in the DeepLab-v3 model. It is performed to refine the segmentation results along the object boundaries. Depth-wise separable convolution is also applied to both estrous spatial pyramid pooling and decoder modules. It helps to increase the speed and accuracy of the encoder-decoder module for semantic segmentation.

For the improvement along the object boundaries, morphological dilation is applied on a void annotation label on the validation set around the object boundaries. After that, mean IOU is computed of pixels that are associated with the dilated band of void labels. More significant improvement is observed when the narrow dilated band is used.

DeepLab-v3+ has improved the Xception model. The following improvements have been made:

- The number of layers has been introduced.
- All the max-pooling layers are replaced with the depth-wise convolutions with striding.
- Extra batch normalization and ReLU activation function are added after each 3X3 depth wise convolution.

DeepLab-v3+ correctly recognizes the subject in the foreground in the picture. In this way, the depth of field and the blurring effect are compatible and perfectly non-artificial. It also improves the method of tagging the pixels using semantics. It can also be used for the segmentation of real-time mobile videos.

DeepMind

DeepMind builds systems that learn automatically. The models are not pre-programmed and the features are not handcrafted. The system is provided with a large number of raw datasets so that the operation can learn from the best representation. In this way, the order is able to operate across a wide range of tasks.

Reinforcement learning architecture is used to develop the systems. The agents generated interact with some environment. The agent takes the actions in the given situation and receives feedback from the environment in the form of observations and further uses those observations to update the behavior of the model.

In the medical field, DeepMind could help clinicians with more accurate analyses and ultimately patients can get faster treatment. The immediate potential analysis helps physicians provide better, faster, and safer care to the patient. The security of patient data is a top priority. Data of patients remain under the full control and direction of the hospital. All information is stored securely and encrypted with the highest standards.

WaveNet

Google DeepMind is developing **WaveNet**—an algorithm that can transform the input text into raw audio. It can show outstanding results as compared to previous attempts.

It is one of the fully convolutional neural networks that contain various dilation factors that allow its respective corresponding field to grow exponentially with depth and cover thousands of steps.

At the time of training, input sequences are original waveforms obtained by recording human speakers. After training, the sampling of data is used to generate synthetic utterances. During the sampling process, the value is extracted from the probability distribution computed by the network. After that, the obtained value is fed back into the input and a process of new prediction is done. The following diagram illustrates the different layers:

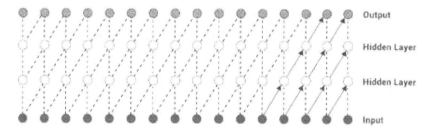

Figure 4.12: Represent ation of different layers

Google also made an algorithm with DeepMind, which is able to read the lips movement of humans.

Tensor Processing Unit (TPU)

Google has made a specialized chip meant to accelerate machine learning applications, that is, **Tensor Processing Unit (TPU).** It supports training machine learning algorithms along with the processing of results from existing models. Cloud TPUs are hardware designed to speed up and scale up Machine Learning workloads programmed with TensorFlow. Every chip can provide 180 teraflops of processing. Google is also able to network the chips together in sets called TPU Pods that allow higher computational gains.

The new chips are helpful in businesses and they'll be able to use them through Google's Cloud Platform. Also, the company is launching a new TensorFlow Research Cloud that will provide researchers with free access to that hardware.

TensorFlow 1.2 includes new high-level APIs that make it easier to take systems built to run on CPUs and GPUs and also run them on TPUs. Sometimes, on the shared computer cluster, there is a need to wait for a job to schedule. Still, with TPU, the user can have interactive and exclusive access to a network-attached Cloud TPU via a Google Compute Engine VM that the user can control and customize.

The online retailer is exploring chips to blink that could lower the cost of production and increase the battery life of other gadgets.

In the field of transportation, Cloud TPUs help to move quickly by incorporating navigation-related data from a fleet of vehicles and the latest algorithmic advances from the research community.

Conclusion

With deep learning, Google is giving another sky to artificial intelligence in the current era of data science. For tackling DL-related challenges, they are not just improving the software part but also hitting the hardware part involved in the implementation of technology. Whether it is giving a special framework to DL by introducing TensorFlow or giving a fully dedicated hardware support to deep learning by developing TPU, Google is handling AI with the use of DL very well.

Questions

1. Discuss some applications under the strategies of Google in deep learning exploration briefly.

2. Discuss the working of autonomous cars briefly.

3. Discuss the working of DQN briefly.

4. Describe the business models that are currently adopted by the company.

CHAPTER 5

Cognitive Learning Services in IBM Watson

This chapter discusses the history of cognitive learning by computers and how IBM utilized the capability of cognitive learning in building Watson. It is an intelligent **Natural Language Processing (NLP)** service provided to encapsulate the complexity of artificial intelligence in developing applications.

Structure

- Cognitive learning in NLP
- IBM Watson
- Improving services with IBM Watson
- Impacting the business with IBM Watson

Objective

- Elaborating and defining the use of cognitive learning in NLP using applications.
- How IBM Watson works and how to make use of the technology?

- Elucidating new potentials in natural language processing, that is, chatbot, and so on.

The cognitive learning in NLP

Natural Language Processing (NLP) is the prime need of any chatbot. If a Chabot has to be fully automated, it needs to use NLP and cognitive computing. Let's discuss these techniques.

Cognitive computing

Cognitive computing is a self-learning system that uses machine-learning techniques to perform specific human-related tasks intelligently. This technology helps to create automated IT models that are capable of solving problems without human assistance.

The result is cognitive computing, which is a combination of computer science and cognitive science. Cognitive computing models provide a roadmap to achieve AI. Let us see the flow of cognitive computing in the following figure:

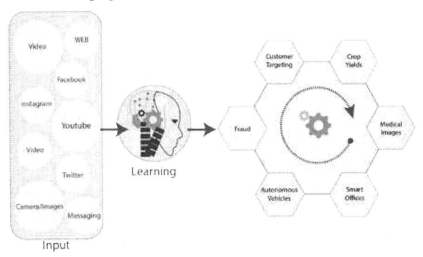

Figure 5.1: Flow under cognitive computing

Cognitive computing is a collaboration of humans and computers to magnify human reason and insight. To extract useful data, cognitive computing systems must be able to learn, iterate, adapt, interact with people, be responsive to them, and understand the information in the correct context.

These abilities allow computers to understand queries raised by humans, suggest answers, and refine those answers from human response and input. The following diagram illustrates the architecture of the neural network used in cognitive computing:

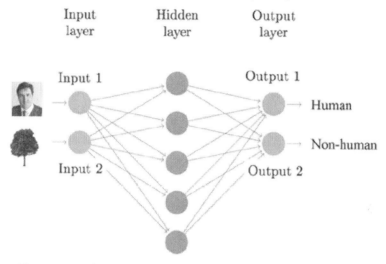

Figure 5.2: Architecture of neural network used in cognitive computing

Big Data growth is accelerating as more of the world is moving towards digitization. Data is increasing in terms of volume, speed, variety, and uncertainty. Also, most of the data comes in unstructured forms like video, images, and natural language.

To handle this, a new computing model is needed for businesses to process and extract useful information out of data and enhance the expertise of humans.

Instead of programming to find solutions to every problem, cognitive computing systems can be trained using AI and ML algorithms that can sense, predict, infer, and think.

Features required for a cognitive system

A cognitive computing system should have the following features:

- **Interactive:** The cognitive system should interact easily with users so that users can comfortably define their needs. It should also communicate with other devices like processors and Cloud services.

- **Contextual:** It should have the ability to understand, identify, and extract contextual elements like syntax, meaning time, location, domain, regulations, user's profile, task, process, and goals. It must work on multiple sources of information, including both structured and unstructured data.

- **Iterative and stateful:** This feature is about the quality of data and validation methodologies to ensure that the system provides enough information and that the data sources it operates on, delivers reliable and up-to-date input.

- **Adaptive:** The system must have the ability to adapt to any surrounding. It needs to be dynamic in data collection and sensitive to goals and requirements.

Evolution of cognitive system

Cognitive computing represents the third era of computing. In the 19th century *Charles Babbage* (father of the computer), introduced the approach of a programmable processor used for navigational calculation. The system was designed to solve polynomial functions. The following figure shows the evolution of cognitive systems:

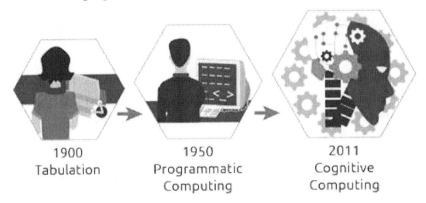

1900	1950	2011
Tabulation	Programmatic Computing	Cognitive Computing

Figure 5.3: Evolution of cognitive computing through different Eras.

The second era (1950) represented digital programming computers such as ENIAC in the age of modern computing and programmable systems. Today, cognitive computing works on algorithms of DL and big data analytics to provide profound insights.

The neural network is the brain of a cognitive system, a primary concept behind DL. A neural network is a combined system of hardware and software that mimics the central nervous system of humans to estimate functions that depend on an extensive amount of unknown inputs.

Characteristics of cognitive computing

Cognitive computing can capture and connect big data so that it can create value from the extracted information while learning continuously because of its inherent capacity to adapt and change. The following diagram demonstrates the significant characteristics that lead to the strategic processing of Big Data:

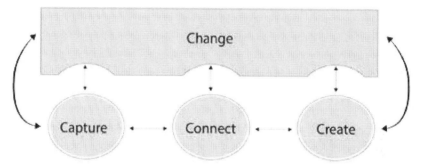

Figure 5.4: *Characteristics of cognitive computing and relationships between them*

Let us discuss the characteristics of cognitive computing and their relationships:

- **Capture:** Cognitive computing can capture vast amounts of data in a single search and store it so that the data is available for analysis. It is capable of self-capturing of multi-structured data. This means cognitive systems can capture more than just data contained in tables; it can capture various images of radiology study, catalog, and more and save them to a database.

  Further, it can tag this multi-structured data to be cataloged and available for use later. Another one of its attributes is that cognitive computing can sense if there are any updates in the data and it can capture the updates.

- **Connect:** An essential characteristic of cognitive computing is connecting multi-sourced data to find new information, and then present that information in a way that is easy to understand.

- **Create:** Cognitive computing can create new knowledge, products, or services. With cognitive computing, new solutions are found and presented in a probabilistic way.

Traditional computer applications require new programs to handle change. Writing new programs takes significant time and costs. With cognitive computing, change happens autonomously as systems continuously learn with algorithms.

Thus, time expensive and expensive updates linked with writing new programs are avoided. Cognitive computing handles change with less help from humans. Moreover, as cognitive systems evolve autonomously, they can keep data up-to-date more efficiently than traditionally programmed systems.

Difference between artificial intelligence and cognitive computing

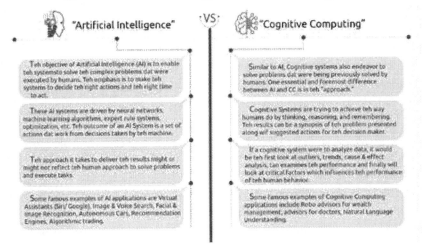

Figure 5.5: Difference between artificial intelligence and cognitive computing

Let's see the detailed difference between them:

- **Artificial intelligence (AI):** The objective of AI is to enable systems to solve complex problems executed by humans. The emphasis is to make the systems decide the right actions and the right time to act. These AI systems are driven by neural networks, machine learning algorithms, expert rule systems, optimization, and so on. The outcome of an AI System is a set of actions that work from decisions taken by the machine. The approach it takes to deliver the results might or might not reflect the human approach to solve problems and execute tasks. Some famous examples of AI applications are virtual assistants (Siri/ Google), image and voice search tools, facial and image recognition tools, autonomous cars, recommendation engines, and algorithmic trading.

- **Cognitive systems:** Similar to AI, cognitive systems also endeavor to solve problems that were previously addressed by humans. One essential and foremost difference between AI and CC is in the approach. Cognitive systems try to achieve results the way humans do by thinking, reasoning, and remembering. The results can be a synopsis of the problem presented along with suggested actions for the decision-maker. If a cognitive system were to analyze data, it would first look at outliers, trends, cause and effect analysis, and then examine the performance and finally look at critical factors that influence the performance of human behavior.

Some famous examples of cognitive computing applications include Robo advisors for wealth management and advisors for doctors.

The scope of cognitive computing and systems

Even though computers are fast in calculations and processing than humans, they have sometimes failed to accomplish tasks that humans have taken for granted, like understanding of the natural language or recognition of unique objects in an image. Hence, cognitive technology offers a new way to solve these problems. Computers equipped with cognitive technology can respond to complex and ambiguous situations that have an impact on personal lives, businesses, healthcare, and so on.

These three capabilities listed below are needed by humans to think and demonstrate their cognitive abilities in everyday life. These capabilities are now mimicked by cognitive systems:

- **Engagement:** The cognitive systems have vast repositories of structured and unstructured data. These can develop profound insights into the domain and assist. The models built by these systems include the relationships between various entities that enable it to form assumptions and arguments. These can rectify ambiguous and self-contradictory data.

  Thus, these systems can engage in detailed dialogue with humans. The chatbot technology is an excellent example of an engagement model. Many AI chatbots are pre-trained with domain knowledge that helps in different business-specific applications.

- **Decision:** Cognitive systems are modeled using reinforcement learning. Decisions made by these systems work from new information, outcomes, and actions. A widespread use case of these models is the use of IBM Watson in healthcare. The system can collect and analyze health-related data of the patient, which includes their history and diagnosis. The system interprets and analyzes queries of complex healthcare data and natural language, like doctors' notes, patient records, and clinical feedback.

  It provides decision support capabilities and helps in the reduction of paperwork that allows physicians to spend more time with patients.

- **Discovery:** It is the most recent and advanced scope of cognitive computing. It includes finding in-depth insights and understanding of the extensive amount of information. These models are built on unsupervised machine learning and deep learning. With the increase in volumes of data, there is a need for systems that help to gain information more effectively and efficiently.

  The distributed intelligent agents in the model help to collect streaming data, like video, text to create interaction to sense, inspect, and visualize the system that provides real-time monitoring and analysis.

Use of cognitive computing in NLP

NLP performs an essential role in cognitive systems as it handles multi-structured data. The main tasks NLP conducts over multi-structured data are as follows:

- Evaluating semantics
- Finding links
- Organizing words
- Giving answers

NLP technologies identify the semantics of words, phrases, sentences, paragraphs, and other grammatical parts in multi-structured data. Cognitive systems combine a knowledge-base of multi-structured data sources. Further, the essential use of NLP in cognitive systems is to recognize the statistical patterns and provide the linkages in the unstructured text that helps to evaluate the meaning of big data in the right context.

NLP refers to a group of technologies that allow computer systems to organize the meaning of words and generate natural language answers. It is a set of methods that find solutions from a knowledge-base. These methods determine the definition of a word, phrase, sentence, or paragraph by knowing the grammatical rules. Furthermore, these methods can extract proper names, locations, actions, or events to find the relationships between and across Big Data.

NLP is a computer system's capacity to make sense of multi-structured data. Processes of the brain are responsible for the understanding of language by spreading activation in semantic networks and providing better representation, which is not possible directly from the text. Therefore, ontologies are used for the identification of specific semantic in the book.

With the use of NLP technologies on cognitive approaches and fewer resource requirements, it is demonstrated as a solution for several practical problems.

Applications of cognitive computing

There are many applications of cognitive computing. It can quickly handle a complex set of tasks involving logical reasoning. Here are some applications of cognitive computing in business:

- **Sentiment analysis:** Sentiment analysis is a science of understanding emotions or feelings conveyed in a communication. It is easy for humans to understand tone, intent, and so on in a conversation, but it is complicated for machines. To enable machines to understand human communication, we need to train the model with data of human conversations and then analyze the accuracy of the analysis. Sentiment analysis is majorly used to investigate the interactions in social media, such as tweets, comments, reviews, complaints, and so on.

- **Chatbots:** Chatbots are programs that can replicate a human conversation by understanding the rules of communication. To make this possible, a machine learning technique called NLP is used. NLP allows applications to take inputs from humans (voice or text), analyze it, and then provide logical answers. Cognitive computing enables chatbots to have a certain level of intelligence in communication, like understanding user's needs based on past conversations, giving suggestions, and so on.

- **Risk assessment:** Risk management requires analysts to go through market trends and historical data to predict the uncertainty involved in an investment. This analysis is related to data trends, guilty feelings, and behavior analytics. As intuition and experience are needed to predict the market's performance in the future, it is necessary to make algorithms intelligent. Cognitive computing helps to combine behavioral data and market trends to generate different insights. These insights can be evaluated by experienced analysts for further analysis and predictions.

- **Face detection:** Face detection is a detailed analysis of an image. A cognitive system uses data like structure, contours, eye color of the face to differentiate it from other images. After the generation of a facial image, it can be easily used to identify a face in an image.

- **Fraud detection:** Fraud detection is another application of cognitive computing in finance. Here, the system is used to detect anomalies. The goal of fraud detection is to identify transactions that don't seem to be healthy (defects).

The challenges faced by supervised machine learning:

- In the case of supervised machine learning, the system learns to recognize thecorrect pattern from labels. Therefore, the problem is to provide a sufficiently labeled dataset so that the system can learn. Refinement of the obtained system has to be performed as therefinement of cognitive reasoning model needs to be improved.

- Another challenge is to balance the system's need for sufficient data and proper human guidance with the objective of training the model efficiently.

- Finally, there is one more challenge of providing the system with defined goals. The system should learn from the obtained outcomes of the implementation after it has had sufficient practice in the dynamic environment.

Issues in cognitive aspects of language modeling

Language modeling is very essential for the integration of cognitive computing and NLP, yet there are some issues in cognitive aspects of language modeling. Let's discuss these issues one by one:

- **NLP and language comprehension:** It is one of the critical issues in the aspects of linguistics and cognitive science. One of the problems is to show the feasibility of the model concerning language comprehension. It also provides information about the language complexity by highlighting the similarity between the linguistic phenomena and the formal devices required to represent them.

  Therefore, the goal of cognitive science regarding language modeling is to analyze the different parts of sentences by different modules and calculate the meaning of phrases that correspond to the various pieces of information stored by these different modules.

- **Language acquisition:** One of the challenges is to have limited and indirect access to the natural regions where a particular language is spoken, thereby impacting language acquisition, language production, and understanding. The process is generally restricted to the outcome of the product. Research studies are moving towards the investigation of different development stages from longitudinal studies. This particular study helps in avoiding any individual bias from personal language traits.

  With the use of simulation in the computational models and the availability of language, acquisition data leads to a higher increase in the in-vitro testing of different theories of acquisition. On the other hand, there is a need to handle noise and ambiguity in the input data while accounting for known language biases via prior probabilities.

- **Clinical conditions:** The concept of graph theory is used for modeling the lexicon as a complex network. It is also useful to determine the characteristics of the system for semantic storage and introduce the changes in mechanism from healthy to clinical networks. Therefore, it is necessary to explore the differences in possible languages using computational methods. There is a need to introduce distributional semantic models that help in capturing the semantic relatedness among the words and successfully explain the human performance in semantic priming tasks.

Cognitive computing landscape

The cognitive computing landscape is influenced by large companies like Microsoft, IBM, and Google. They invested billions of dollars in Big Data and real data analytics and now spent an estimated one-third of their R&D budget on the development of cognitive computing technology. Now, even new companies are investing heavily in this technology to develop better products.

The following diagram shows various companies that are investing in this technology:

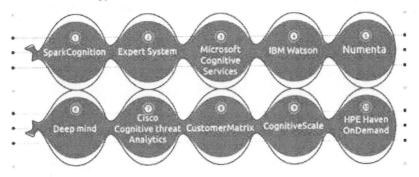

Figure 5.6: Various companies that are investing in cognitive computing.

IBM Watson

IBM Watson is a platform that deals with computing. It works from its ability to interact in natural language. It can process vast amounts of data. It can learn from each interaction. It can understand massive amounts of big data at variable speeds to help professionals in understanding data quickly while increasing knowledge over time.

Watson is a cognitive system that analyses through libraries of data to discover insights. These in-depth insights can help users answer the most complex questions directly. IBM Watson leverages detailed content analysis and evidence-based reasoning to accelerate and improve decisions, reduce costs, and optimize outcomes. Watson uses a set of transformational technologies that leverage natural language, hypothesis generation, and evidence-based learning.

Watson understands the problem of human language. It can bring relevant answers back in the context of the question. It also gets smarter, learning from each interactionwith its users and each piece of data. It is not a deep learning model that requires data scientists to predict and interpret results. However, it does much more.

Watson can think or answer in a way similar to the human brain. It processes raw information, concludes, and learns from its experiences. Watson does not use inbuilt rules and structured queries to find answers. Instead, it generates hypotheses based on a wide variety of relevant information. Responses express recommendations along with confidence rankings. Unlike a traditional analytic tool, it receives more data, learns more, and provides higher quality insights.

Organizations are currently using business analytics to discover new insights into their performance and identification of future opportunities. However, systems can also transform the way humans think, behave, and operate. In today's era of cognitive systems, orders are able to learn through experiences, create hypotheses, find correlations, learn, and remember the outcomes.

Watson solutions

IBM Watson is the environs of cognitive computing capabilities. There are several critical areas of innovation, some are as follows:

- **Watson Explorer Platform:** The framework of expandable cognitive indexing and natural language search.
- **Watson Developer Cloud:** A collection of APIs that can be used in applications.
- **Watson Industry Solutions:** Health, IoT, marketing, supply chain, education, banking, financial services, regulatory compliance, surveillance, insurance, and many more.

IBM Watson Explorer

This topic provides a high-level overview of the IBM Watson Explorer modules. It is used to create 360-degree information applications. It includes information about the various logical components and capabilities of Explorer Engine, the interaction between them, and the security when exploring enterprise information.

Watson Explorer Engine provides a modular and flexible architecture. It interacts with the network data repositories and network-accessible data sources. This architecture simplifies the creation of a single navigation information application. The application can easily explore the content stored in various formats and at different locations.

It includes the formats that are unique to applications. It also consists of the combination of different formats that are found in networked repositories. Watson Explorer Engine helps to explore data from repositories by creating an index of the document. There are many ways to create an index of the text from a single data repository:

- Crawling repositories means to retrieve data, metadata, and security information from the pool. Whenever there is a difficulty in crawling a deposit, Watson Explorer supports server-side applications that push data to a Watson Explorer installation from a data repository.

- For processing and augmenting the retrieved data, the data must be in the standard format. The data should be in a standard form like URL with which it was linked, the original file type, and permission information.

- Creation of index of the data.

The following diagram shows the various functional components of the Watson Explorer Engine, interaction, and external data repositories:

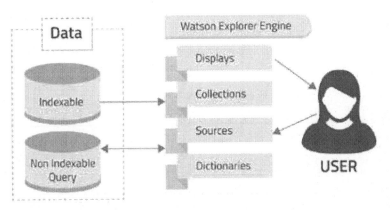

Figure 5.7: Various functional components of Watson Explorer Engine, interaction, and external data repositories

The preceding diagram shows their use in information navigation and searching of applications. The next few sections describe the components of the architecture of Watson Explorer Engine in detail:

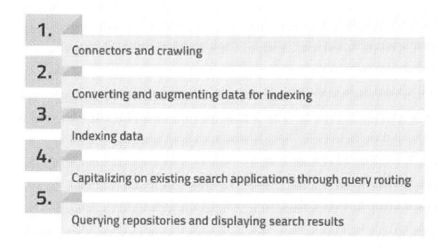

1. Connectors and crawling

2. Converting and augmenting data for indexing

3. Indexing data

4. Capitalizing on existing search applications through query routing

5. Querying repositories and displaying search results

Figure 5.8: Components of the architecture of Watson Explorer Engine

The following points describe the components of the Watson Explorer Engine architecture:

- **Connectors and crawling:** Watson Explorer Engine can access and index any data using Universal Resource Locator. Watson Explorer Engine has provided connectors to locate and retrieve the data in remote repositories. URLs for each data item are retrieved in the data repository and enqueued to the Watson Explorer Engine using a component known as the crawler. The crawler retrieves the data from each enqueued URL and passes it to the corresponding metadata. The extracted data is used for subsequent preprocessing using the other component known as pull connectors. These connectors are responsible for retrieving both URLs and data from remote repositories.

  Another method to crawl the data from remote repositories is to install the server side component known as push connectors. These connectors directly enqueue the datafrom remote repositories. They are very useful for those repositories that do not offer suitable API or when the crawling is impossible or insufficient.

- **Converting and augmenting data for indexing:** After the identification of data by URL and retrieval by the crawler from the remote repository, it is handed over to the series of applications known as converters. These converters are used for the normalization and also augmentation, if required. The data retrieved by the crawler is in a particular format as per the corresponding repository. Therefore, the indexer is necessary to understand all these formats. This results in an increase in complexity, and it diverts its focus towards indexing. Also, changes are needed to the indexer to enable indexing for the previously unseen document.

Indexing should be accurate and quick so that it can focus purely on indexing rather than transformations. Extracted data is to be normalized and converted into one specific format that is used internally by the Watson Explorer Engine. It is performed by processing the data using a sequence of connectors known as conversion pipeline.

In the conversion pipeline, the respective converter converts the data from one format to another or performs augmentation if required or even adds the information in the input data before passing it into the next converter. There are two combinations of connectors available such as:

o **Standard converters:** They are broadcast with the Watson Explorer Engine.

o **Custom converters:** They are written by the Watson Explorer Engine to extract and augment the data in the specific format.

Each converter is composed of input and output types. Only those converters in the conversion pipeline are activated, which match the characteristics and features of the initial input data and output data of previous converters.

The conversion pipeline is also responsible for following a predefined sequence. It authorizes the augmentation process of specific data and follows the format of conversion by other converters that support the same type of input:

o The standard format internally followed by the Watson Explorer Engine is known as **Vivisimo XML (VXML).** It is a well-documented and composed of less schema data syntax.

o It is comprised of multiple attributes for each retrieved data. It is responsible for preserving the metadata by content associated with the original repository.

o It can split the data that correspond to a single URL into multiple splits to provide the information of the structure and composition of the original data. This helps in processing and indexing the data differently.

o Converters can also be used to add un-searchable metadata for display purposes only.

- **Indexing data:** Watson Explorer Applications use an index for data exploration and information navigation. It is a profoundly difficult job to look into each remote repository to extract specific information. Therefore, there is a requirement of simultaneous exploration of multiple indexes. It provides various advantages such as:

  o Improvement in the optimization of numerous processes like connecting and fetching data from remote repositories, standardizing, augmenting, and indexing from input data. It results in improving the performance by creating and updating a specific index.

  o Reduction in the size of the given index. This feature helps in reducing the immediate and infrastructure storage requirements.

  o Reduction in the time and resources which are necessary for accessing the data within an index.

To meet the **reliability, availability, and serviceability (RAS)** requirements of Watson Explorer Engine, indexes can be configured to enable their replication across multiple Watson Explorer Engine installations. It is known as **distributed indexing.**

The updates in all replicas are automatically distributed to other models by the change of content in the associated data repository. We need to perform the index synchronization transactionally to fortify successful and steady updates across all index replicas:

- **Capitalizingexisting search applications through query routing:** There is a potential for combining the search results from existing search applications with the data exploration and navigation abilities of Watson Explorer. The process is known as query routing. It is used to navigate the exploring queries to theexisting search applications and towards the content indexed by the Watson Explorer Engine. It helps to allow access to all available information across the 360-degree information applications.

Watson Explorer Engine applications use a component known as the source for accessing both indexed contents and existing search applications. This source component is responsible for having fine-grained control over the matching data to be returned and processed. Whenever an exploratory query is navigated to the existing search applications, the source component can identify the process of submission of the question to that particular application. The source also diagnoses the prioritize process and paginates the information obtained from the search application to combine the results of exploring indexed content successfully.

- **Querying repositories and displaying search results:** The data obtained as a response from the source component is formatted and shown in the web browser by a Watson Explorer Engine component known as the display. All these displays are created in the Watson Explorer Engine administration tool.

Working with Watson Explorer

According to the developers of Watson, advanced generation of hypothesis and scoring combined with deep NLP and ML capabilities are the qualities that make Watson unique. The working of Watson Explorer is elaborated with the help of the following points:

- When a query is generated, Watson analyzes the issue to determine the type of information that is needed, such as a person's name or location, age as well as various possible interpretations of the question and the evidence that supports it.

- Watson searches across its knowledge repository for several possible answers to the problem and possible explanations. It forms hundreds or thousands of predictions around the answers and gathers the evidence that supports them.

- Watson performs in-depth comparisons between the different language of the question and the response using reasoning algorithms to score the hypotheses it made.

- Using advanced analytics algorithms, Watson merges the comparison scores individually to generate a final confidence score for every possible answer andranks them accordingly; it then provides the user with the highest-rated answers. The following diagram describes the flow of Watson Explorer:

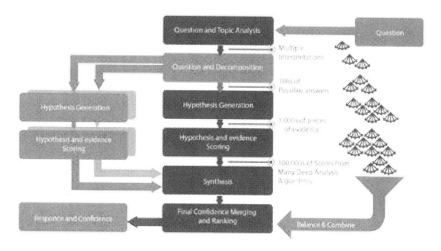

Figure 5.9: Flow of the working of Watson Explorer

- The confidence score of Watson can improve over time by interactions with those users who train the system.

Some of the benefits of Watson Explorer in business are:

- **Improvement in the performance:** The business benefits of Watson Explorer are not bound to a single department or within an organization. It gives broad access to information across the entire enterprise, and it is able to deploy targeted 360-degree informatics applications in departments or across functions like market intelligence, customer care, or supply chain visibility.

- **Increase in customer lifetime value:** Watson Explorer enables the organization to provide marketing, sales, and professionals of customer service with a 360-degree view of each customer and product. It gives them up-to-date information and the knowledge they need to increase their performance. Advanced Edition of Watson Explorer helps organizations with content mining and analyzing unstructured content to detect patterns. It provides a better understanding and anticipates customer behavior and needs.

- **Support compliance and reduce risk:** Watson Explorer makes policy-related information accessible. It is helpful in the implementation and enforcement of information governance policies. Compliance officers can quickly identify and track potentially hazardous information easily, such as breach of personal data. It is a useful tool to make audits less labor-intensive. Also, users can implement a more in-depth analysis of unstructured data to reveal patterns and trends with the help of the advanced content analytics capabilities of Watson Explorer Advanced Edition.

- **Content mining for in-depth insights:** Advanced Edition of Watson Explorer helps to analyze and mine unstructured content to identify ideas that would be difficult to generate otherwise.

- **Information sharing:** In today's distributed environment, everyone stays isolated and loses the opportunity to interact with their colleagues. Watson Explorer offers many ways to help your colleagues by developing information through tagging, rating, and commenting on content.

- **Gain knowledge from existing information:** Sometimes, valuable data and insights are locked in such a way that it is challenging to have a proper search and navigation capability. It is also tricky to integrate with other information systems. If the organization can extract value, it is helpful to gain the opportunity to leverage existing investments without costly migration and replacement projects. Watson Explorer can enhance transparency in research and development and reduces the time-to-search.

Improving services with IBM Watson

InfoSphere **Master Data Management (MDM)** from IBM is a portfolio of product offerings that cater to two different MDM domain styles: single-domain and multi-domain. With InfoSphere MDM, organizations can create single and trusted views of data that help to increase the efficiency of processes and facilitate better decision making. This section describes the services that IBM customers gain by capitalizing on MDM on Watson Explorer. It is broken into various segments and covers a specific industry in each part.

Government

The government-industry is broken down into two functional areas:

- **Public safety:** Public safety consists of military, law enforcement, and intelligent customers who are hired to ensure security and stability along with the awareness of threats and the ability to prevent crime.

- **Citizen services:** Citizen services deals with the state, local, and provincial governments, and the services that they provide.

Government agencies demand from taxpayers to access information intelligently. For instance, some person who is involved in a home-building project does not want to give detailed information to the local planning commission initially to obtain permission from the relevant departments. Those departments should be able to access information of people harmlessly.

In other words, citizens also expect the same type of integrated service from government agencies that they receive from service companies. By integrating Watson Explorer with MDM, governments can access complete citizen-centric information that provides government services the flexibility to collect and share information quickly.

With the use of Watson Explorer, the government can view the current, accurate, and complete picture of citizens and business information, and respond to constituent needs in real-time. Both citizens and governments save time and money and increase taxpayer satisfaction.

Citizens can gain the following advantages:

- Engage in dialog with officials.
- Access government information and services quickly.
- Provide instantaneous feedback on issues and topics.

Law enforcement

In the past, 95 percent of criminal activities were local and could be easily be tracked at a fixed location, but now times have changed. Criminals are mobile. They are using technology to reach beyond geographical boundaries. To fight against globalized crime effectively, law enforcement agencies also need to use technology in new and different ways. Information sharing across authorities can help law enforcement agencies to be ahead of criminals and find them irrespective of where they operate from.

However, adequate information sharing requires that the data provided by an agency is accurate, and kept secure throughout the sharing process. It also assumes that the providing agency can still control the information one agency shares with another. Without these conditions for security, information cannot be shared across agencies. To provide the relevant and updated information to the officials, there is a need for a consolidated view of each entity associated with an investigation. MDM offers a unified view of suspicious activities from multiple sources in real-time.

MDM analyzes massive amounts of information from a variety of sources, including criminal reports, arrest records, prison reports, and court filings. MDM models the data by creating a multi-entity view that can include any of the following entities:

- Person
- Locations
- Property (weapons, mobile phones, automobiles, and so on)
- Events (robberies, assaults, murders, and moving violations)

It is then able to find relationships within this information by identifying the patterns or commonalities. By integrating Watson Explorer with MDM, law enforcement agencies can empower their officers by incorporating unstructured data from social media into the information already provided by MDM.

MDM helps organizations accomplish the following tasks:

- Identify suspects
- Track suspects
- Improve cross-jurisdictional cooperation
- Control the amount of data shared and with whom it is being shared

Financial services

The financial services industry refers to both banking and insurance institutions. This section describes the management needs of these institutions.

Banking

The primary focus of banks is to build customer relationship and product information fragments across multiple systems. Without an authentic master record of their customers and products, banks will struggle to provide consistent and relevant services across all channels sell the most suitable products to customers or reduce operating expenses.

MDM of Watson Explorer enables banks to execute this strategic objective by making core information available across the enterprise to support business processes. Customers want to interact with their banks in different ways. Individuals no longer communicate with a single local branch. They also do business on the web and mobile applications.

Banks should ensure that local branches, customer representatives, and online systems can access all customer information that is collected through all previous interactions. It provides an excellent experience for customers that reduce attrition and drive new sales. MDM also helps banks to recognize customers from multiple systems and provide customers with a complete view of their assets. The result is a consistent experience for the customer, whether they bank at a branch, online, or on mobile devices. Also, banks can use MDM for reducing costs, streamlining customer information processing, simplifying client on-boarding and setting up new accounts, and eliminating duplicate mailings.

Insurance

For attraction and retention of customers, insurance companies put customers first. Building strong relationships and understanding the needs of customers is essential to reduce churn and increase the number of products used by each customer. Companies dealing with insurance must keep up with the changing pattern and be the preferred choice of their customers. Nowadays, customers want more ways to interact with insurance companies.

Insurance companies must ensure that local agents, call-center agents, and online systems can access all historic information collected during previous interactions, to provide a seamless experience for customers, thereby reducing attrition and generating new sales.

As customer information is scattered across multiple and disparate systems, it is important to bring customer information together in one place. This strengthens customer relationships, helps companies sell more products during customer interactions.

For example, if a customer contacts a call-center to discuss some insurance policy, and the agent has no information about the customer's previous interaction with another local agent, the customer will have to spend time repeating the information. MDM brings together customer information from across business channels, policy lines, and service locations. Further, it creates a single and centralized record for each customer that helps to improve business processes and application efficiency.

The single record can be any of the following types:

- A physical record, in which the history of the customer is maintained in a centralized hub.
- A virtual file, in which changes to customer information are made through individual policy-based systems.
- A hybrid record, in which only some part of the document, is centralized.

In this way, MDM gives insurance companies the flexibility to manage customer data.

Healthcare

Creating a single and centralized record of each patient can help healthcare organizations with the following benefits:

- More collaboration among healthcare providers.
- Consistent patient experience across multiple points.
- Reduction in medical errors.
- Enhancement in efficiency of patient processes.

Integration of information from multi-sourced systems helps to ensure proper routing of patient information among physicians. Organizations must create an up-to-date record of providers and facilities that cover a wide range of internal and external data sources.

MDM helps organizations improve the quality and accuracy of critical documents through effective management of the patient and provider data. Effective management of patient and provider information can deliver immediate benefits and return on investment. With an accurate view of the patient, organizations can establish a patient-centric approach that boosts the care quality, streamlines processes, and improves patient satisfaction.

For example, the following improvements can be achieved in the field of healthcare:

- Improvement in healthcare provider collaboration.
- Elimination of duplication of effort.

- Availability of patient information to healthcare providers at the point of care for treatment.
- Reduction in administrative costs and complexity.
- Avoidance of safety issues that occur due to incorrect patient information.

With a foundation of high-quality and accurate data, healthcare organizations can implement such a solution that helps to increase the meaningful use of this data for the benefit of patients, providers, and organizations. Also, applying analytics to patient and provider information can help organizations identify factors that contribute to successful patient outcomes. With this, there is an improvement in the effectiveness of treatment.

Retail

Master data is necessary for organizations to deal with outdated, incomplete, inaccurate, and unsynchronized information. An organization's primary business processes depend on master data. Without complete trust and accurate master data, the operations are compromised and become inefficient.

MDM of Watson is designed to help organizations address the complexities of master data, which includes how data is created, updated, used, managed, and analyzed. With MDM, organizations can centralize critical data by creating a trusted source of information and a single view of each customer. It provides a wide range of MDM functions, which includes adding, deleting, validating, updating, and securing access to the master data.

Customer domain

Integration of MDM with Watson Explorer brings together customer information from communication channels which include social media sources helping retailers can quickly build a 360-degree view of each customer. Retailers can use that unique customer view to create personalized marketing campaigns and promotions.

For example, a product-seller that sell products online can create a personalized promotion strategy by creating categories of products that a customer has recently bought or shown interest in, based on the online activities of the customer. With a detailed record of a customer's searches and purchases, retailers can accurately generate recommendations for other products.

By creating detailed customer records, Watson Explorer helps to integrate social media and other internal and external data. It helps retailers reduce expenses and create better marketing campaigns. With the elimination of duplicate records and with the creation of personalized campaigns, retailers can enhance the productivity and efficiency of sales efforts, thereby improving the success rates.

Product domain

A centralized source for product information is essential to provide customers with the correct information like when, where, and how they want it. For example, customers buying an air conditioner are expected to do the following:

- Visit a physical store.
- Use a manufacturer's website.
- Shop at a retail e-commerce site.
- Compare prices on a smartphone.

Delivering information across different channels helps to produce a specific retail experience, which inspires confidence and loyalty among customers. Retailers might need to accomplish the following tasks to centralize product information:

- Collect product information from a manufacturer.
- Translate that information into an understandable format.
- Deliver that information to sales and marketing teams.

This process is time-consuming and leads to errors as information is entered into the systems repeatedly. Using MDM, the retailer may create a centralized source of product information. It will be available to all users that may work inside and outside the organization. With this single source of information at a centralized place, the retailer may save time and money.

How to impact businesses with IBM Watson

Businesses from various industries can benefit from Watson Explorer. This platform is built on a natural-language analytics engine. The explorer was designed to be extremely flexible and adaptable and help improve a wide range of business processes. The best way to understand this is to see how Watson Explorer is assisting companies in solving their most significant challenges in several sectors.

Watson Explorer for manufacturing

As manufacturing techniques become more interconnected and intelligent, manufacturers need access to even more data. Watson Explorer helps the manufacturers to extract value from their data by identifying patterns and trends. It also enables access to information across teams. It can also help increase productivity, innovation, efficiency (while reducing time), staffing redundancy, and risk.

Watson Explorer drives the main improvements for manufacturers i.e. improvement in business processes and development in products. It can lead to the following tangible benefits:

- **Reduction in investigation and recovery costs on defects and product quality:** By identifying defective products and production equipment on time, analytics solutions can help minimize the impact of these errors.

- **Better market position and reputation due to stronger product design and quick correction of defects:** Product designs can be safer and more remediated along with more receptive to customer preferences and feedback. A better product is the best way to improve customer satisfaction.

- **Reduced risk of defective products:** By minimizing or avoiding the number of defects that make it to market, companies can reduce their exposure to legal liability and customer dissatisfaction.

Watson Explorer for customer service and call-center

Call centers are a significant challenge for data-driven analytics. Customer call centers provide an expensive and high-touch process that involves a massive volume of unstructured data. The reputation of a multinational company can be affected by the service provided through call centers and customer engagement channels.

Watson Explorer creates a workspace for customers facing professional problems and other decision makers. It analyzes structures such as supply chain management, customer relationship management, and unstructured content from sources such as file shares, email, and content management systems. The benefits for call centers can be dramatic and far-ranging:

- **Reduced average handling time and increased call resolution:** Watson Explorer helps to enhance efficiency for call center agents by successfully integrating data from multiple sources. It then applies analytical tools to get a 360-degree view of a customer and provides call center agents with relevant information.

- **Improve application performance and accuracy to handle daily operations and business users at different sites:** Call center agents can attain a holistic view of customers and get efficient access to vast volumes of previous customer and product data.

Watson Explorer for retail and e-commerce

Retail and e-commerce organizations need to gain in-depth insight into unstructured and individualistic experiences and optimize the store inventory to maximize revenue and profits. Cognitive analytics can help in this process. The benefits of cognitive analytics in retail relates to understanding the customer better. Cognitive solutions can help retail clients in the following ways:

- Changing stocking patterns for stores to match the products that are selling
- Reduction of supply chain and logistics costs
- Identification of trends and checking the products are in-stock and visible
- Prediction of customer orders months in advance

Watson Explorer for insurance

Insurance companies deal with unstructured data and have an interest in building long-term relationships with their clients. Nowadays, most clients of insurance companies use cognitive services that help to reduce the time needed to process claims from two days to 10 minutes. These companies are using data to identify hundreds of millions of dollars in leakages and fraud. The result is more a customer-centric and profitable company. However, any new technological solution needs to balance contradictory aims like updating and improvement in current on-site search capability.

Fortunately, Watson Explorer can balance all these concerns. It enables search across the public website and the corporate intranet. It helps with predictive search and high priority content identification. Some identification steps which are used in the process:

- **Identification of fraud and leakage:** The first step to eliminate fraud and waste is to identify when it occurs. Watson Explorer can find patterns and relationships in data to help insurers identify fraudulent claims more efficiently.

- **Reduction in call center response time:** Improving call center responsiveness is a simple step that can improve both customer satisfaction and profits.

Conclusion

Cognitive computing is still recognized as a synonym of AI which is not exactly right; it should be considered as the sub-part of AI. To achieve full autonomy in the field of chatbot, a combination of cognitive Computing and NLP techniques are required. Questions like how to make that integration, what will be the requirements, what will be the challenges, and how it can affect different areas and sectors, can be answered fairly from the mirror of IBM Watson.

Questions

1. What is cognitive computing? What are its prime features?

2. Explain the working of Watson Explorer.

3. State some benefits of IBM Watson in business.

4. State the differences between artificial intelligence and cognitive computing.

5. Discuss the architecture of Watson with its components.

CHAPTER 6

Advancement of Web Services by Baidu

In this chapter, we introduce **Baidu** which incorporated intelligent capabilities for the advancement of web services. This Chinese company is leading the AI space and taking web services to the next level by introducing DL in most of its products and services. It can be seen as a potential game-changer by Silicon Valley's giants including Google and Facebook.

Structure

- Baidu web services and its business orientation
- Deep learning in Baidu web services
- Next steps of Baidu intelligent web services

Objective

Understand the web services provided by Baidu and the potential use of deep learning in improving user experience. We'll also discuss the use of deep learning in different cultures and nations.

Baidu web services and its business orientation

Baidu is the largest search engine in the Chinese language used in China. It was created by *Robin Li* in *January 2000*. According to Alexa, it is at number 5 in the world in terms of traffic. Baidu states that more than 90 percent of Internet users in China use Baidu with millions of searches every day.

Baidu provides a variety of search products, such as maps, book search, mobile search, image search, and many more. In various ways, it is similar to Google's search products, but there are many differences in how ads are displayed and managed. Like Google, Baidu has an advanced pay per click marketing platform.

The main aim of Baidu is to give customers:

- An online marketing platform to meet their marketing needs
- An extensive selection of tools for managing their accounts
- Data for analyzing and optimizing ROI

Baidu is a web services company that provides many services. One of its essential services is its search engine. It also offers other services like Baidu Baike (a service that is similar to Wikipedia) and Baidu music.

It is the most efficient and well-designed search engine in China. Baidu is controlling 70 percent of the Chinese market. Therefore, it is difficult for other search engines to look for geographies to penetrate as it provides the services to customers in allgeographies in China. Every online business person in China has to market their services and products on Baidu to grow their business. The following diagram illustrates the market share of Baidu:

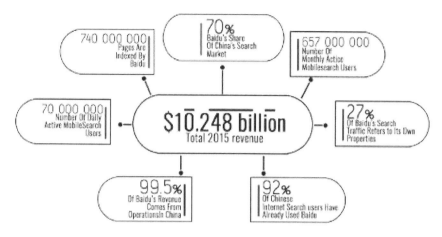

Figure 6.1: *Market Share distribution of Baidu*

Market share of Baidu

Baidu is the most comprehensive search engine in China in terms of revenue and market share. With the arrival of new competitors in the market and an increment in the number of internet users, there is a need for Baidu to be alert and focused. The following diagram shows the market shares of web search platforms in China:

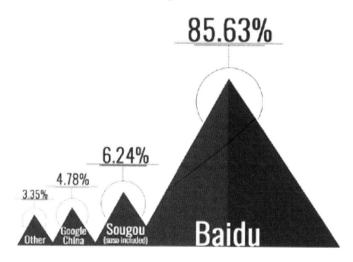

Figure 6.2: *Share distribution of Baidu*

It is clear from the above figure that it is mandatory for all the industries in China to advertise their products and services on Baidu to spread their messages to 85% of the users.

Baidu plays a similar role in China as Google plays in the U.S., but it has a broader market share as compared to Google. The total revenue of the company in the second quarter of 2016 was $2.748 billion, a 10.2 percent increase compared to the same period in 2015, and a 16.3 percent increase year-on-year. Simultaneously, mobile revenue accounted for 62 percent of the total revenues for the second quarter of 2016 as compared to 50 percent for the same period in 2015. Net income assigned to Baidu in the second quarter of 2016 was $363.2 million, a 34.1 percent decrease obtained from the corresponding period in 2015.

In 2016 Baidu lost some reputation due to the allegations of false advertising information regarding the medical domain. Therefore, to enable a favorable online ecosystem, Baidu started focusing on limiting the advertisements aids and allowing higher standards of advertisers. By posting new regulations, it is expected to have significant growth in aid revenue.

Tools for Baidu

Baidu provides various tools to improve online traffic. Here's a brief introduction of the available tools:

- **Submit website tool:** This tool is used to handle the changes made in the Baidu website. Baidu does not consist of a sitemap submission feature. Therefore, there is a need to re-submit the website each time any significant change is made. If the user does not use the tool, then Baidu will not be able to recognize the changes made on the website, resulting in poor ratings for the site.

- **Keyword search tool:** Keyword search tool should be efficient enough for Baidu. Searching habits are different for different types of users based out of various locations. This tool provides information about the most prominent keywords, and it lets users select the most appropriate keyword with optimum value. If the user selects a highly competitive keyword, then the user has to work extremely hard to achieve a high rank on the first page of the search results. On the other hand, if the user selects a less competitive keyword then the competition will be extremely low, and the website will not appear on the first page as it is not searched frequently. Therefore, it depends upon the selection of keywords.

- **SERP layout tool:** This tool is used to decide the layout of web pages and show the results web pages after any web search. The format of the result page (SERP) is very much similar to the Google search engine. However, Baidu filters out the primary paid results on page 1 and its particular web ventures. Baidu consist of various projects, therefore, the organic results are placed at the top. It includes *Baike, Zhidao, Wunku, Tieba.*

- **Baidu open tool:** There is a stage where the user can build applications by feeding their data. This tool is used to enhance the result outputs. The tool is not able to affect the organic searches; instead, it chooses to show the results of the gadgets by keywords used. The popular devices comprise vertical searches or weather predictions. It results in good practice for the development of the business as it offers new online opportunities.

- **Baidu brand zone tool:** This tool is also known as the brand zone. It provides access for brands to buy their trademarked keywords so that they can control the rules regarding SERP of branded terms. The results obtained may be composed of media such as tabbed, back linked content, and many more. Due to the large size of obtained outcomes, a change in the appearance of SERP is observed. The position of the advertisement in the brand zone on page 1 is a tough job for a large competitor's brand.

- **Brand landmark tool:** It is a tool that is used to grasp the information more specifically as compared to the brand zone. The brand zone is very useful to determine the association of particular trademarked terms, whereas the brand landmark tool is helpful for accessing more generic names. It is highly beneficial for corporations and medium businesses.

- **Baidu's content requirement tool:** The main task of this tool is to maintain the quality of the content. A higher quality of content is required to improve the ranking. Therefore, to determine the quality of content every search engine has its standards. Users understand those particular standards to maintain their position over their competitors. Specific requirements are provided by Baidu to evaluate the quality of content. If users follow those requirements efficiently, their webpage will rank high on SERP without paying a dime to Baidu.

- **Plagiarism checking tool:** This tool is used to check plagiarism in content. Baidu penalizes websites with plagiarized content. The content of every site should be unique. Therefore, one should be careful while building the site. There are numerous issues associated with plagiarism such as taxonomies, legal issues, and more.

- **Language usage handling tool:** All the substances and Meta tags are composed of simplified Chinese characters. Baidu works for improving simplified Chinese characters over the traditional Chinese characters which disfavor the Romanized nature. This is because younger people identify the new simplified symbols and characters quickly. Therefore, it is suggested to stay away from those traditional characters that are no longer considered as mainstream. A large number of blogs and websites are available that provide the list of regular characters and symbols to avoid.

- **Content definitions tools:** The Chinese language consists of various styles. Every word of the language represents different meanings. Therefore, it should be verified that all the words used in a website are used correctly.

- **Content quality checker tool:** Baidu strongly depends on the quality of the content and the amount to be published for ranking. Baidu has a minimum standard value of 300 words for each page on a site. Frequent users can extend the number of words, but the optimum standard value of the number of words should be present on each page of the site.

- **Title tagger tool:** For the composition of the title tag, a limit is provided. For writing with familiar Romanized characters, the limit is up to 70 characters. Whereas, the threshold for writing simplified Chinese characters is up to 35 characters. Rich keyword expression should be utilized for writing title tags.

- **Meta descriptions:** Baidu uses Meta description as a tool for the determination of ranking. There may be a possibility that a Meta description is composed of a couple of keyword phrases with branded terms. The limitation of Meta description for the Romanized character is 156, whereas, for simplified Chinese characters, it is 78.

- **Meta keyword tags:** Baidu uses keywords for the computation of rankings. They are used on each page of the website and are composed of 3-4 keyword phrases. Users should stay away from keyword stuffing.

Difference between Baidu and Google

There are some critical differences between Baidu and Google Search Engine, which are as follows:

- **Ease of search:**
  - o **Baidu:** Whenever users click on the search engine page, the corresponding page opens in a new window or tab. This feature allows the user to come back to Baidu, which results in increased click-through-rates. Therefore, it enables users to access multiple web pages on the result page of their specific search query.
  - o **Google:** It is not the same case for Google. In Google, if users open the webpage, it will redirect them to the selected page, and the user has to leave the previous page. Therefore, if the user wants to view results in multiple web pages, they have to open pages manually in a new tab or window.

- **Click through behavior:**
  - o **Baidu:** Baidu uses the click-through-rates feature for the computation of rankings and, further, the results are clicked on. It is also responsible for recording the number of users who come back to SERP to search for the other results. They can be used to fetch the best results to distinguish and observe the different clicking behavior of users.
  - o **Google:** Google does not any have click-through-rates-feature; instead, Google uses PageRank algorithm which is developed by Google itself. According to this algorithm, important pages are ranked high and they appear at the top of the search results.

- **Fresh content:**
  - o **Baidu:** Baidu gives more importance to the freshness of the content on a website. Therefore, Baidu offers an excellent opportunity to SEO experts for new projects.
  - o **Google:** Google prefers the power of the page. But on Google, it is difficult to replace the big companies even with a significant amount of data and content as the

power of the page is fixed. Google users know the results of some keywords in advance which makes them less interested. But Baidu page results keep changing due to the introduction of fresh content and its originality.

- **Quantity over quality:**
  - o **Baidu:** Baidu focuses more on the number of links rather than the nature of links. Therefore, to improve ranking on Baidu, the website should contain as many backlinks as it can, as the relevance of backlinks is not as important.
  - o **Google:** On the contrary, Google puts considers the quality of the links to be more important.

- **Requirement for speed:**
  - o **Baidu:** Baidu also focuses on the loading time of the website in its positioning algorithm. Therefore, the websites should host companies that offer fast speed servers. It is recommended to have a dedicated server to make the site faster rather than having shared servers.
  - o **Google:** Google provides the functionality to check the speed; it is known as *PageSpeed Insights* which shows the speed field data for a given site. It also provides suggestions for optimizations to improve the websites.

- **On record:**
  - o **Baidu:** Recording of the pages by Baidu is very challenging as compared to Google. Baidu takes information from users regarding hosting and geographical locations to register for their database.
  - o **Google:** Google is composed of a system that automatically stores the pages in the database with more general rules.

Business model of Baidu

Baidu's services include pay for performance, algorithmic search, enterprise search, and a host of specialized services that include news, multimedia, and image search. The main focus of Baidu is a Chinese language search engine service which is its biggest advantage. Let us look into the main points of the business model of Baidu:

- **Customer segments:** Baidu provides a range of search platforms explicitly for the Chinese-speaking population. It operates the most popular search services in China, which accounts for around 88 percent of the site's web traffic. Within the Chinese-speaking community, Baidu serves consumers and internet users. In addition to serving general consumers, Baidu also provides marketing and advertising services to brand marketers and advertising agencies.

- **Value propositions:** Baidu's most significant value is that it provides a wide range of web search services that are used for an audience that speaks Chinese. The company has a variety of services and portals that enable users to integrate their accounts across multiple different channels. These channels are accessible from anywhere through mobile, web browsers and mobile apps. Baidu provides a set of search tools that cover a broad area of interest and needs, from legal searches to news portals. Baidu also provides a platform to a large audience which includes advertising agencies and brand marketers, helping them expand their marketing reach and interaction with their target audiences.

- **Customer relationships:** Baidu offers a wide range of self-service products. Users can access the company's web portal, as well as other services, without registration of an account or interaction with members of the Baidu team. Advertisers can inquire regarding paid search and display of advertising campaigns by contacting Baidu directly and receive personalized service according to their needs. The following diagram illustrates the relationship between Baidu, users, and clients:

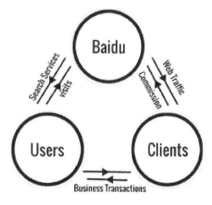

Figure 6.3: Relationship between Baidu, users, and clients

The company also provides support to its customers through FAQs and user guides, and it interacts with them through social media accounts, like Facebook, Twitter, and China's Sina Weibo.

- **Channels:** Baidu operates an online portal. The company also operates various proprietary websites for other services that include **http://d.nuomi.com/, https://www.hao123.com** and **www.news.baidu.com.** Baidu also operates its application store by which customers can easily download Baidu and other third-party applications. The functionality of Baidu is also integrated into a range of websites and technology products.

- **Key partners:** Baidu collaborates with technology partners and integration partners. The Company also has tie-ups with high-profile multinational companies like Amazon, which helps them power the Amazon Kindle Fire in China; and Microsoft, which supports the promotion of Windows 10 software to Chinese consumers. Baidu has also partnered with web performance and security companies named *CloudFlare* and web discovery platform, *Taboola*. It has also associated itself with performance marketing agency *Merkle*, and *BMW* to develop driverless cars in China.

- **Key activities:** Baidu is a web search company that works with Chinese technology. It provides a wide range of Chinese-language search products that are organized around its central web portal hosted at **www.baidu.com**. In addition to its search engine capability, the company also offers the following platforms:

  o Baidu Post Bar, which is a Chinese-language query-based online community platform.

  o Baidu Knows, which is the world's largest interactive knowledge-sharing platform in Chinese-language.

  o Baidu Encyclopedia, which is the world's largest user-generated encyclopedia in Chinese-language.

  o The company generates its revenue from digital advertising and marketing solutions. Baidu also operates a network of technologies, integration, and affiliate marketing partners.

- **Key resources:** The critical resources of Baidu are its online platform, technologies, and IT infrastructure. Baidu has various patent applications with the US Patent and Trademark Office. It includes an applications-entitled method and apparatus for monitoring the state of the online application, method and system for pushing the point of interest information, and a display screen with a graphical user interface.

- **Revenue streams:** Baidu generates more revenue through online display advertising and digital marketing solutions across its websites and its affiliated network. The company operates a pay-for-performance advertising platform. It functions efficiently as a web-based auction system that allows customers to bid for priority placement of advertisement links. The company uses a *Comprehensive Rank Index* which gives priority placement to relationships based on bid prices and a link's quality score, which is generated by calculating the relevance of the relationship against a user's search query. Charges are applied on a pay-per-click basis. Customers can also be charged on the basis of the number of telephone calls that are directed to them as a result of their advertisements. Further, Baidu offers paid search services. In this, a customer's link is placed at the top of a search with the help of selected search terms.

- **Cost structure:** Baidu earns from research and development, marketing and traffic acquisition, IT infrastructure maintenance, retention of personnel, and bandwidth. The company collects human costs through its workforce which consists of more than 43,000 employees and operational costs that include rental and utilities concerning its offices across Japan, USA, Thailand, China, Egypt, Brazil, and Indonesia.

Product strategy

Baidu provides a number of products that promotes two specific functions:

- **Baidu Post Bar:** It is the discussion board engine that is useful for users to scan information regarding their specific topics, post discussions, and participate in the community. It also provides the provision to start thread discussions and connect with the users who have purchased a specific item. It also determines IWOM companies, as users use it to write reviews with positive and negative sentiments. It is located where users can gather online and exchange reports.

- **Baidu Zhidao:** It is one of the question-answer features of Baidu search engine. It allows users to ask questions and receive output as an answer. The users are mostly from rural areas who are excited to know about various new technologies and their working. The members of the community answer questions pertaining to any particular field. The following three factors are responsible for its significant growth in the rural markets:
    - o Usability of services
    - o Cost efficiency
    - o Ease of use

The feature is very useful in delivering information easily and free of cost.

- **Baidu Baike:** It is a community-based encyclopedia similar to Wikipedia. It allows users to edit information regarding any subject. This feature engaged the population of China to collaborate and develop some innovative things that are expected to be beneficial for the entire country. It is highly successful in China as it allows users to develop, and it shows their progress based on their contribution towards the community.

Get the best ranking in the Baidu Search Engine

The following steps need to be implemented to get a good rank in the Baidu Search Engine:

- The basics of SEO should be adequately implemented, such as title tags, Meta descriptions, and keywords.
- Proper optimization of anchor text for internal linking matters.
- It is preferred to write the content of the website in the Chinese language rather than the English language.
- Submit the website to the Baidu trend, if the indexing of the site is left behind.
- Good quality links in high quantity numbers should be present on the website.
- Having the server located in China is an excellent way to get a better rank.

Research and technology

Here are the components on which Baidu invest its research and technology:

- **Baidu Big Data Engine:** Chinese search engine Baidu has opened its big data engine officially; it provides massive storage, cloud computing analysis, and a deep understanding of research technologies to the outside world. The three modules of Baidu's big data engine are an open cloud, data factory, and Baidu brain.

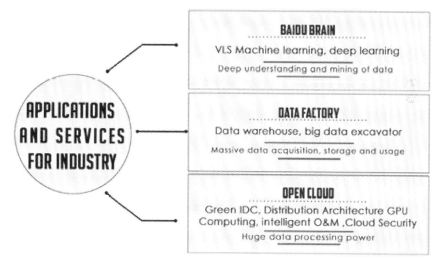

Figure 6.4: Different components of Applications and Services for Industry in Baidu

With the big data engine, Baidu's cooperating organizations will be able to use Baidu's big data structure via the internet. Meanwhile, they can also use Baidu's big data technologies to improve enterprise management and business model links in traditional industries.

- **Baidu Big data enabled intelligent systems:** Baidu is a company with world-class expertise in every significant AI area: speech, NLP, computer vision, machine learning, and knowledge graph. The following diagram illustrates the different areas related to Baidu's Intelligent Systems:

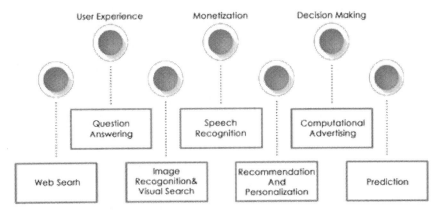

Figure 6.5: Different areas related to Baidu's Intelligent Systems

Baidu is the early mover in AI research in China, and it concentrates on fundamental research in deep learning, leveraging its exploration in Big Data, like Google. Baidu already deploys technology to enhance critical products including core search algorithms, voice recognition engines, recommendation systems, and other mobile app products. It is powered by its large-scale cloud data centers, as well as GPU-embedded servers.

- **Baidu brain research:** With the emergence of technologies such as blogs, social networks, IoTs, and cloud computing, data and information on the internet are growing and expanding at an unusual rate.

  As we are moving towards the 22nd century, with the advancements in technology and a large amount of available data, everyone wants to adopt online systems for every task. Interactions between users on the internet, information from enterprises and governments, and the real-time information from the IoTs sensors are generating tremendous amounts of structured and unstructured data at all times.

Such data is scattered throughout the internet network system in a considerable volume. The data contains precious information on economy, science and technology, education, and so on. Such data can be used to make a prediction system that can predict the future. The following figure illustrates the flow of Baidu Brain Search:

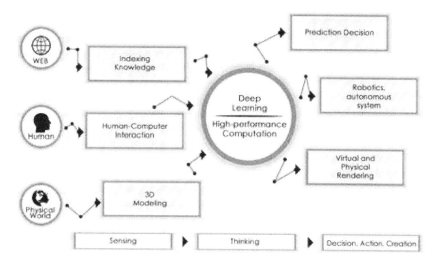

Figure 6.6: *Flow of Baidu Brain search*

Virtual reality technologies are used for creating life like 3D environments for activities such as swimming; people can feel as if they are physically in the scene in a swimming environment. Baidu was also researching intelligent robotics and intelligent manufacturing technology as an entry point to greet the new industrial revolution.

Nowadays recommendation systems are also popular in many industries like online retail, e-commerce, and so on. The most common use of recommender systems in retail is to find customers who are most likely to buy similar items after they buy the first item. The system acts as a salesman who can give suggestions to customers by understanding their taste, style, and so on, and help them make buying decisions.

SWOT analysis

The following diagram illustrates the SWOT analysis of Baidu:

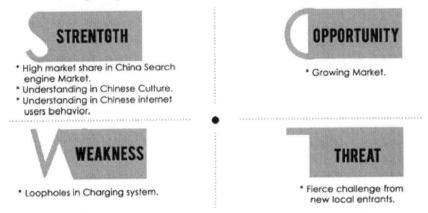

Figure 6.7: *strengths, weaknesses, opportunities, and threats in SWOT analysis*

The strengths, weaknesses, opportunities, and threats in a SWOT analysis of Baidu are discussed below in detail:

- **Strength**
    - o **Market share:** Its biggest strength is the market share that it has. As of 2015, Baidu had a market share of 79.81 percent. This is a massive market share. With such a vast market share, it is difficult for anyone to challenge it.

    - o **Mobile users:** Baidu also provides services to mobile internet users. Nearly 54 percent of its revenues come from mobile and internet users. Baidu has around 657 million active mobile users every month. Its real strength comes from users who are very hard to match.

    - o **Brand equity:** As of 2016, Baidu is ranked 86th in terms of Brand equity. Apart from China, Baidu is used in many other Asian countries as well.

    - o **Listed companies:** Baidu is the first Chinese company that is included in the NASDAQ 100 Index. Its in-depth knowledge of search algorithms and customized catering for the Chinese make it a brand name.

- **Weaknesses**

    Baidu has the following weaknesses:

o **Brand recall outside China:** The main weakness is the lack of brand recall outside China. There are very few people who have even heard of Baidu. The company needs to work on this. It cannot remain restricted to China.

o **E-commerce business:** The e-commerce business of Baidu is considered separately from the company and lost out in a potential market that could help the company to grow bigger.

o **Smartphone industry:** The company entered very late into the affordable smartphone industry. An earlier entry would have ensured a better market share.

- **Opportunities**

o **Paid search and advertising:** Google has a significant share of the paid search and advertising segment because of its AdWords and AdSense programs. However, Baidu paid search is far behind globally; however, it can reach its true potential with some more brand awareness.

o **Capitalizing on market share:** The considerable market share in China gives it a great opportunity to become the most significant technology and web services brand in China.

o **Infrastructure:** Its existing IT infrastructure is strong, and this can be used to expand its services in China. With excellent servers and IT systems in place, it cannot be beaten by its competitors.

- **Threats**

o **Presence of healthy players:** The presence of more prominent players in the market is a significant threat to Baidu's growth outside China. Players like Google, Bing, and Facebook are active players and have a tremendous amount of market share in the global market.

o **Wikipedia:** Baidu has a service known as Baidu Baike which is an encyclopedia, like Wikipedia, but the recognition of this brand outside the Chinese market is very less.

o **The speed of innovation:** Considering the rate or speed at which technology-oriented companies are innovating, Baidu has to work hard to stay relevant in the business. Companies such as Google have much more money than Baidu, thus, their speed and extent of innovation significantly differs from that of Baidu's.

o **Government intervention:** In this type of business, the government enforces rules and regulations on the functioning of a search engine. A governmental control can hamper the operation of Baidu's search engine, which a source of significant income.

Deep learning in Baidu web services

Baidu is currently considered as the leader among the Chinese internet giants as it is ready to develop and deploy machines and deep learning technology. AI methods such as ML and DL are used to reap enormous benefits across industries such as finance and healthcare. The basic idea is that once computers are taught to learn, they will be able to absorb the data in the same way and process it in the form of Big Data at a tremendous rate.

Over the past few years, there has been a rapid evolution of DL algorithms. It has played an integral role in improving the accuracy of several applications including image recognition, speech recognition, text to speech, and machine translation. DL models used in these apps are continuously emerging due to fast growth in AI research.

To support the computing needs of deep learning, new startups and large companies are building innovative hardware and software systems. Building hardware systems is an expensive and time-consuming process. The changing nature of in-depth learning research makes it difficult for hardware manufacturers to develop systems that can meet the needs of applications that use deep learning.

Baidu's DL technology has made excellent progress in various challenging tasks, such as image processing, computer vision, NLP, and so on. In the age of big data, one integrated Spark platform using scalable in-depth learning, training, and prediction is essential, especially to Baidu scale.

Let's discuss comprehensive learning, training, and prediction using Paddle, a deep learning library developed by Baidu IDL. It enables multiple Baidu productions, such as offline processing to do data ingestion, pre-processing, feature extraction, and model training in one Spark cluster.

DL had many use cases in Baidu and showed significant improvement in quality:

- **Image retrieval ranking:** Baidu image search engine is the search engine of the People's Republic of China. It is a **content-based image retrieval (CBIR)** search engine. Different from traditional image search engines, it matches a user query keywords with the surrounding text of images and enables users to use an image as the query directly. By simply uploading a local copy or pasting the URL of a web image into the search box, users can quickly get access to many web images that are similar to the query. Besides, it also displays stories, news, knowledge, and additional web information about the queried image.

- **Ads CTR prediction:** Click through rate is a crucial metric for advertising. It is the ratio between the number of clicks on an advertisement and the total number of impressions. Improving CTR improves revenue. Also, a high CTR means more relevant ads on the page which can indirectly be improving user experience as well. A standard way to optimize CTR is to predict the CTR of a profile of ads with several features about a user, such as the page, the ad itself, and many more, before actually displaying the advertisement. Another way is to choose to display the ad with the highest CTR.

- **Machine translation:** As the most significant Chinese search engine, Baidu has released its machine translation system. It supports translations to and from 27 languages on multiple platforms, including PC, mobile devices, and so on. A Hybrid translation approach is essential to build an Internet translation system, as the translation demands come from various areas which include news, patents, poems, and so on. It is difficult for a single translation system to achieve high accuracy in all areas. Therefore, hybrid translation is needed. Baidu built a **statistical machine translation (SMT)** system that solves the problem of machine translation. To make people communicate in a foreign language, the Baidu translate application supports various ways of translations, such as speech-to-speech translation, image translation, object translation, full-screen translation, and so on. Object translation helps users to identify objects and translate them into both Chinese and English. For the users who cannot speak and write foreign languages, the app allows images as input.

- **Speech recognition:** Baidu has developed a voice system called Deep Speech 2 that can readily recognize English and Mandarin speech better than humans. AI is prevalent throughout Baidu's business lines. It impacts its significant products, such as search, advertising, translation, and online-to-offline services, which include restaurant recommendations. The company owns a supermassive neural network built upon hundreds of thousands of servers, and it also has the largest GPU group in China. The company focuses on the commercialization of AI technology across its new AI-enabled business initiatives, such as cloud, autonomous driving, financial services, and DuerOS, all of which have the potential to become Baidu's core businesses.

Key assets of Baidu

The key assets of Baidu are as follows:

- **Baidu Intelligent Cloud:** It consists of AI and Big Data, that is, ABC - AI, Big data, cloud computing. The newly launched platforms for Baidu open cloud customers are as follows:

  o **Baidu TianXiang:** It is an intelligent multimedia cloud that offers video, image, and document processing services, such as live streaming and video-on-demand.

  o **Baidu TianSuan:** It is an intelligent Big Data platform that offers data services and cognitive APIs, where users can collect, store, process, and analyze Big Data.

  o **Baidu TianGong:** It is an intelligent IoT service that offers full-stack stop and smart IoT services for users in several industries, such as energy, logistics, automotive, and retail.

- **Baidu Brain:** It acts as the core engine of Baidu AI and helps in the development of many Baidu technologies, such as voice and image recognition, natural language processing, and user profiling. The following diagram illustrates the architecture of Baidu Brain and Intelligent Cloud:

Figure 6.8: Architecture of Baidu Brain and Intelligent Cloud

- **DuerOS:** It is a conversational platform that provides the voice interface service in various smart devices both at home and on the go, such as phones, intelligent speakers, TV, cars, robots, and many more. The critical elements of DuerOS are as follows:

  o **Accurate listening:** It is one of the first and crucial steps of the interaction. It has the Deep Speech to speech recognition system. The system includes a noise reduction algorithm and has achieved a maximum of 97% accuracy.

  o **Understanding:** The goal of DuerOS is to understand the free writing style of user comments. Baidu aims to provide consistent user experiences in which buzz-words and stylish slang can be used in commands along with an interactive system that can only understand pre-defined words. Its skill is supported by its substantial data assets and market-leading technologies, which include NLP and searching.

  o **Fulfilling:** It fulfills the needs of customers with the ability to offer complete content and services. Baidu has use cases of interactive conversations, which include entertainment, information inquiry, chat, smart home, travel/transportation, phone instructions, personal assistant, utility tools, and education. The content and services provided by DuerOS overgrow on a daily basis.

Figure 6.9: Architecture with contents and services provided by DuerOS and their flow

- **Apollo:** Security, reliability, and real-time control: Apollo is open-source software, which provides free self-driving services. With this, Baidu aims to engage users with its open-source AI platform. The following diagram illustrates the architecture of Apollo:

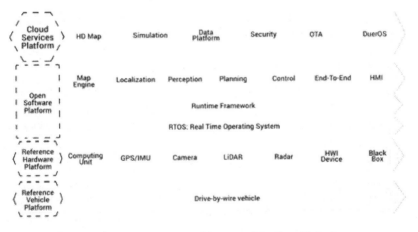

Figure 6.10: Technical architecture of Apollo with its flow

- The complete technical architecture is composed of the following four parts:
  - o Cloud Service Platform focuses on security, reliability, and real-time control by Simulation Engine and HD Map.
  - o Open software platform consists of the following:

- The perception, which can help vehicles recognize road conditions with the help of AI technology.
- Localization, which can correctly locate the position of the car in a low-cost and uninterrupted way with the support of Map Engine.
- Runtime Framework, which can use chips of both Intel and NVIDIA.
- Planning and control, which can choose the safest driving strategy with the help of AI and Big Data.

o Reference Hardware Platform provides support for various hardware,such as CPU, GPU, and a variety of sensors that include GPS, camera, and laser.

o Reference Vehicle Platform can prevent and investigate accidents by using data from the black box of Apollo.

Uses of Baidu

The following are the uses of Baidu:

- **Core business:** The core business of Baidu is the online advertisement feature in its search engine. The principle behind this service in Baidu is called **Pay for Performance (P4P).**

- As both Baidu and Google service is based on pay by click, they have different advantages and disadvantages. In Baidu, the paid link is on the left side and mixed with the search result. When customers pay, they will be precisely told where their link will be placed according to the price they pay.

- Another advantage of Baidu which comes from its prosperous localization approach is the personal service. When the customer registers as an advertisement user on Baidu, the local sales team contacts the customer and comes to the portal to offer assistance. For those people who don't want to make an online payment, this is very helpful. This approach brings many SMEs to Baidu.

- **MP3:** The MP3 searching and downloading service is the primary tool for Baidu to get users to click on advertisements. But this has led to a lot of discussion on legal issues and copyright. Consequently, Baidu came up with a solution and offered only those third-party links that are announced by Baidu on its website.

- **Knows:** Baidu Knows is a platform that helps people to interact with each other with questions and answers to each other. The advantage here is that people can find what they want quickly and precisely, instead of wasting time in hundreds of search results.

- **Post bar:** It's an open BBS system. The main difference between these systems and standard BBS is that every user can start a new topic and be an administrator. So, it is commonly used by schools to setup classmates BBS, or clubs for singers or football teams, and so on.

- **Space:** It's a blog system. Users can quickly start their homepage that can include their blogs, photos, and links to their friends' pages.

Major problems of Baidu

The following sections describes are the major problems related to Baidu.

Uncertain quality of search results

With the spread of internet users, many businesses focus on the development of mobile websites. According to a recent study, comparison of keyword searches through mobile advertisement is two-thirds of the overall advertising.

Most users prefer to search for different keywords on mobile devices, and the cost of the mobile advertisement is less than that of a desktop. The mobile promotion ranks web pages depending on distinct searching habits and the quality of search keywords. The mobile advertising is only suitable for mobile devices and it works on the pay-per-click model.

The display character and form of searched results will be more suited for the cell phone screen. Furthermore, some are concerned about the traffic flow. As the conversion ratio of mobile search is higher, the cost-per-click decreases and the consulting channels such as *Baidu Shangqiao* are available for use.

Problems in Baidu mobile promotion

- **Invalid mobile search:** The delivery of a keyword in Baidu mobile is lower than the minimum display price for its keyword promotion. The low bid causes the inconsistency in mobile search i.e. two different rates and degrees of keyword quality for the same keyword. It may generally lead to invalid promotion, and the keyword gets displayed on Baidu mobile only after an appropriate adjustment.

- **Low click rate on the impressions from mobile devices:** With the popularity of smartphones, the mobile search capacity is also increasing. The search volume from mobile devices is three times that of desktops, but the conversion ratio of searches from portable devices is lower than that of desktops. It may lead to several problems for users, such as user's limitation of the mobile screen size, and usually, only three locations are accessible on the heads of a mobile device, while there are ten of them on desktops. Besides, the clicks and impressions on web pages would increase by considering the online behavioral habits of users, promotion delivery location and time, and whether the titles, descriptions, and pictures are attractive enough, assisted by direct calls and online consultation. Firstly, applications have the highest priority, which may not appear simultaneously with other impressions, and secondly, phone calls have the second most top priority, which may appear simultaneously with other impressions.

- **Malicious clicks from mobile devices:** Everyone who engages in Baidu promotion is facing this problem of malicious clicks, which is used to suppress competitors. Some companies repeatedly click on a webpage to decrease the advertising effect of a competitor. Doing so may waste a competitor's money, reduce their ranking, and affect them in other ways, which in turn will reduce the competition cost. To trace malicious clicks, there is a need to check the increase of daily clicks on a keyword, the rise of daily consumption, or excessive clicks from one IP.

- **Under-performance of mobile promotion:** Since mobile browsing behavior is irregular, the browsing behavior tends to be fragmented. Firstly, the user has no time to analyze the advertising information or to decide whether to buy a particular product or not. Secondly, the screen size of a mobile device is limited, which means that product information may not be fully displayed. Thirdly, user experience in mobile devices is poor in terms of real-time communication; this may lower the user's interest in consultation and affect the promotion effect. Lastly, many companies use large-size pictures on their sponsored ads. The user chooses to avoid such ads since domestic data usage rates can be expensive.

- **Copyright problem:** Copyright owners have synchronized with the libraries for a long time, but the digital environment has broken this agreement. Copyright owners are doing everything to preserve the authenticity of their products. In the initial stages of internet development, no one believed that regulation of using online products is going to be a problem, but the internet encountered growing efforts as it emerged.

  For the digital library, traditional copyright has become an obstacle to further development. It is a critical problem at the time for China's digital library suppliers. Copyright is the central concern of the digital library resource reconstruction. To solve these copyright infringement problems, China's significant digital libraries suppliers are seeking useful and practical solutions.

- **Baidu Wenku: a copyright dividend model:** Baidu Wenku is an open platform built and managed by Baidu for internet users to share online documents. Baidu does not edit or modify the content. The first model is the shared fee model. Baidu allows users to read some chapters of the works for free. In case a user wants to read the full text of the document; they are asked to pay a specific fee through specific internet banking channels. After paying, the user can store a soft copy of the work in the *My Library* section on the platform and read the complete content online. The fee charged by Baidu is shared with the copyright owners. Baidu confirms that a significant proportion of the revenue will be transferred to the copyright owners.

  The second model is to share advertisements revenues. Baidu allows users to read the full content for free. Baidu puts corresponding advertising alongside the content users are interested in, in such a way that the user's reading experience is not interrupted. Baidu also provides comprehensive digital copyright security schemes. Firstly, with advanced anti-piracy technology, Baidu erases the residual data from the library thoroughly and restricts the pirated content. Secondly, as long as the designated users report piracy, Baidu agrees to react to it immediately and erases the pirated content instantly.

Next steps of Baidu intelligent web services

Here are the different next steps of Baidu intelligent web services:

- **Make more valid promotion by optimizing the keywords:** Baidu Search has set strict requirements for the degree of keyword quality and the bid for keywords. When the bidding of a keyword is lower than the average price for impressions, the information is not displayed. It also refers to an invalid promotion, which means that the bid of a keyword should be higher than the average price for impressions. There is a lot of commercial software used to modify the amount of keyword software. For example, adSage is designed for Baidu backstage accounts, which allows for the automatic configuration of the display location of each keyword, impression price, and bid area. After the configuration of keyword location and the effectiveness of a bid, it reconfigures the setting of this keyword.

- **Improve the information impression by regional website optimization:** Mobile promotion is preferably done in local user searches, like when a user searches for a tourist attraction. Baidu Search displays lvmama.com on desktops, in which it shows a list of Wenzhou local tourist attractions on mobile devices.

- **Mobile users tend to search some questions with an immediate solution:** Where is a parking lot nearby? So, in this case, the location of target customers is the critical point; the user can identify the areas during a period of advertising campaigns.

- **Prevent malicious clicks by backstage settings:** As to the malicious clicks in Baidu promotion, the company may select the precise keywords, or set a limit by summing up the average daily consumption for each keyword. The promotion cost is reduced by setting a different limit for each keyword and lowering the rank. Baidu backstage setup program also blocks the IPs that are considered as the source of malicious clicks.

- **Understand the customers, optimize the website, and improve ROI:** Before mobile promotion, there is a need to understand the target customers. The searches cover a wide range of areas; more customers already close the promotion information before they get to know the products or services of a company.

A promotion campaign should take a high rank by price advantage if the impression of a keyword attracts more clicks. The company may raise the bid for that particular keyword. Also, companies should change the delivery time and areas depending on their target customers, through the analysis of their searching behaviors. For the mobile business sites, the company profile on the web page should be precise and intelligible to target customers, so that user experience is enhanced. The number of words on the page should be more readable and creative; some appealing GIFs may be added to attract more customer clicks.

The business communication software of Baidu clearly states that customers are required to leave their mobile number for the convenience of follow-up contact. This is particularly essential for follow-up customer tracking on mobile devices.

Conclusion

This chapter described the strengths, weaknesses, opportunities, and threats of Baidu in the field of web searching. Though it is not used in most countries throughout the world, with the power of AI, Baidu is on the way to becoming a giant in the world of internet searches. Till 2017, the number of Baidu users stood at 731 million. Baidu is still exploring AI and its applications, and it is on the way to provide some exciting new internet searching services, which we discussed in this chapter. The day is not far when it will become an open challenge to Google and other search engines of the world.

Questions

1. What is Baidu? What is the difference between Google and Baidu?

2. Discuss the next steps of Baidu intelligent web services.

3. Discuss the major problems of Baidu.

4. What is SWOT analysis? Discuss the same with respect to Baidu.

CHAPTER 7

Improved Social Business by Facebook

Introduction

Social media is the most revolutionized technology ever made in human history. This chapter introduces the role of Facebook in engaging and connecting people by establishing networks of users in the whole world. The chapter also emphasizes the effort of the company in focusing on the research and development by establishing **Facebook Artificial Intelligence Research (FAIR),** which is responsible for making the networks of users more efficient, to be used and utilized.

Structure

- The impact of connecting people
- The current progress of FAIR for advancing social media
- Potential use of deep learning in improving customers among social media users

Objective

- Understand the use of deep learning in social media
- Learn how to leverage massive data using deep learning technology
- Improve customer experience by connecting people

In the last few years, the trend in global business has been the adoption of new marketing strategies that utilize the advancing technology applications available today. One of the leading technology applications used in business improvement is the use of social media. Social media has appeared as an internet-based platform which is incredibly dynamic and vibrant. It is the platform where one user can communicate with hundreds or thousands of other users. Nowadays, social media has been the most recent and booming technological innovations. It extends a wide range of benefits in different fields.

In the current modern culture, social media channels are commonly used to connect people throughout the world. Social networks, forums, blogs, or media sharing websites help people to have an online conversation, also known as an interactive dialogue, with anybody on any topic and at any time. Social media allows users to share their own experiences and valuable information. At the business point of view, social media marketing has offered a variety of new opportunities that help companies to promote their brand, products, and services.

Advertisements over the last few decades have been changing rapidly. Reaching consumers has become much more comfortable for companies with the availability of new technologies. Social media websites also offer various tools and applications that could significantly help to increase the growth of small businesses and non-profit organizations and can be more cost-effective. Social sites can be used to network with organizations and assist employees in finding employment and give corporate advice to business professionals.

Social media websites can also provide extensive opportunities for industries, which was difficult for most organizations to obtain on their own. Companies were offered a new platform of advertisements that has great potential to change the way they present their products and services to consumers. Companies can establish an image of innovation that can address generations of all ages.

The main advantages of social media are shown in the following diagram:

Figure 7.1: Main advantages of social media

Let's look at them one-by-one:

- **Sharing of ideas:** Social networking websites allow users to share thoughts, events, activities, and interests within their networks. Web-based social networking services help to connect those people who share benefits and activities across political, economic, and geographic borders.

- **Bridges communication gap:** Social media bridges the communication gap between different people. It offers stable platforms to online users. Users can easily find other users who share the same interests and build communities based on those shared interests. With the availability of technologies and services, content sharing and user interaction has become easy and efficient.

- **Important marketing tool:** Social media is used by most organizations for marketing. Companies use social networking sites to generate ideas on the current and future products that are available in the market. It is an excellent marketing strategy undertaken by companies to attract consumers and obtain public opinion. Such ideas or comments are helpful for the organization to redesign their products. In other words, social networking is an essential way of promoting products and generating ideas.

- **The tool of communication:** Teachers and learners are frequently using social networks as a communication tool. Teachers create chat rooms, forums, and groups for classroom discussion, posting assignments, tests, and quizzes. Learners can also form groups over the social networking sites and engage in conversation on different topics over a variety of issues.

- **Important customer interaction tool:** Social media networking is excellent for customer feedback, customer interaction, and customer support. New business contacts can be easily obtained for networking purposes.

- **Source of information:** Content generation and sharing sites act as sources of information for various topics. Users can search for any content, download, and use the available content on these sites free of cost.

- **Important crisis communication tool:** Social media can also be used to communicate with the public regarding any crisis.

Introduction to Facebook

Facebook has changed the lives of billions of people and creates significant economic impact. Facebook was started in the year 2004 by *Mark Zuckerberg* as a social network for the students of *Harvard University*. Within the University, Facebook was visualized as an interface to connect with a number of friends and provide space for promoting ideas and interests openly.

The vision of Facebook is to make the world a more global and open space and grow to be one of the largest online communities in the world. Facebook had expanded the general population by 2006. It has improved the experience on mobile platforms and promotes the connectivity to grow in developing markets. Therefore, with the expansion, Facebook provides new opportunities to permit the economic impact within and outside of its platform.

The percentage of people engaged on the platform increased in the year 2014. In this way, Facebook is successful in representing the largest audience altogether on the single platform in the world.

Facebook provides the platform for businesses of all sizes and technical culture. Therefore, the users get the opportunity to speak directly with the corresponding customers. As a result, now Facebook is a hub and an open platform for marketing.

The following are the advantages of Facebook:

- **Facebook is free:** Facebook provides free services to its users. It has a well-designed website and can engage the users for the longest time. In recent days, some paid services have been started by Facebook, but those paid services are not compulsory for its users, and the users have the freedom to choose the right service.

- **Facebook helps in networking:** Facebook helps to connect with school friends, college friends, and relatives. Also, Facebook gives opportunities to its users to make new friends from different parts of the world. Facebook users can use various services such as Facebook chat, poke, messages, group, and many more to connect with different people and improve their relationships with them. Therefore, the users of Facebook can take advantage of the various services provided by Facebook and maintain their relationships. Instead of only sharing videos and albums, they can write blogs, articles, and share it with their associates.

- **Facebook promotes business:** Facebook has billions of users across the world; therefore, it is the best place for companies to promote their products or services. Using Facebook, companies can enhance their brand value in the social media network. Companies can direct their products or services through promotional drives to their target audience over Facebook. For acquiring business, organizations can make a Facebook fan page of their brand or company.

- **Facebook as image and video hosting site:** Facebook users can create albums of their pictures or videos on Facebook and share it with all or just friends or keep it isolated by using Facebook privacy.

- **Facebook video chat:** Facebook's video chat tool allows its users to video chat with their friends and relatives. Facebook has an inbuilt video chat application that offers the service of video chatting to users.

- **Free gaming and app store on Facebook:** Facebook provides free gaming services to its users, where the users can play games with their friends. Also, Facebook offers open application store where the user can use various Facebook applications.

- **Facebook security:** Facebook has exceptionally high standard privacy policies, and it provides high-class protection to the users. The privacy settings of Facebook are simple; so, the users can efficiently use them to secure their account. The users can easily hide the posts of the spammers, block them, or report them to Facebook.

- **Facebook for news:** Facebook is used by many users as a source of information and news.

Effects of Facebook on third-party business

Economic and econometric modeling is used for analyzing the effects of Facebook on third-party business. The analysis covers different aspects:

- **Marketing effects:** It is used to determine the estimation of impact on the use of Facebook for business purposes. Facebook acts as a marketing tool to drive offline and online sales and also increases the awareness of the brand. It provides a set of products to connect businesses and people, such as pages and targeted advertisement. With the use of pages and aids, business people can adequately acquire and retain customers and increase the awareness of the brand. People can also search for companies and brands and connect with them as per requirements. Besides, government, nonprofits, and other civil society's organizations also use Facebook to get in touch with their respective members and constituents. Three sources of effects are available to create the economic impact of marketing such as pages, targeted advertising, and referrals. Let's discuss them in detail:

  o **Pages:** They are used in the business to enhance and establish their presence online across tablets, mobile phones, and desktops. People can locate pages from Facebook according to their interests.

  o **Targeted advertising:** It targets by the characteristics of the audience of Facebook. It allows marketers to send messages at a large scale to their most relevant customers. As a result, returns are increased on advertising. Targeting the right audience is essential for enabling cost-effective advertising for businesses.

Further, by aggregating all collected insights during the respective advertising campaigns allow the markets to fine-tune their campaigns further. Facebook provides self-service feature so that marketers of all sizes can utilize auction-based aid tools to create campaigns at a large scale. The features can lower the barriers to advertising. In this way, these features are highly useful for those marketers who are not able to promote their products and services in the traditional channels.

Facebook has also provided the provision of sharing links to friends, to whom the user is connected. Sharing of links is highly beneficial for creating the significant impact on sales and fundraising which can be considered as a good marketing strategy. For example, Facebook has helped to spread awareness among people regarding the Ice Bucket Challenge in which the challenger has to take a bath from the ice water bucket, and he/she can forward this challenge to any other person, which resulted in a cyclic effect of this whole challenge. It resulted in a significant increase in the donation for the treatment of ALS, which should be considered as a positive marketing effect.

With the use of Facebook's mobile application for the integration of advertisement, it allows marketers to connect with people regardless of the device used. Further, the marketer takes advantage to spread the high popularity of the Facebook application. Moreover, businesses can also utilize their online presence to obtain their customer feedback, crowd source ideas and enroll potential employees.

This way, Facebook is beneficial for marketers to reach their customers and spread their business nationally, globally, and locally. Furthermore, it allows generating a significant economic impact regardless of company size, location, industry, or technical sophistication.

- **Platform effects:** Platform effects are responsible for the estimation of economic impact from third-party products and services building at the top of the Facebook platform. The Facebook platform provides the developer's application with compelling opportunities for discovery and monetization of their application. It further enables economic activities and jobs. The products on the Facebook platform allow the developers to customize their application by taking the person's permission. These features are especially powerful for gaming applications. Further, it has led to the development of new jobs and innovations of social gaming in the travel and music industries.

- **Connectivity effects:** Connectivity effects create economic impact through Facebook by motivating the use of internet and purchasing devices. Innovation in mobile devices and internet infrastructure and the number of services built on top of them are facilitating the sharing of multimedia content. For example, users on Facebook shared HD video captured by mobiles, post links to stream music.

To access these services, customers have to buy high-speed internet and more data. Simultaneously, due to advancement in computing that includes faster processing power, more realistic graphics accelerate a cycle of innovation that developers leverage to create applications on Facebook. The change in technology motivates people to buy new and powerful mobile devices with high power consumption.

Connectivity in countries allows people to take part in the digital economy, stimulates economic impact, and enables the transition to the knowledge-based economy.

Benefits of social media in businesses

In this chapter, we will analyze benefits found by businesses while implementing Social Media Marketing strategies. The main benefits described will be lead generation, brand exposure, targeted traffic, market insightsthat market research, and competitor monitoring, and many more. Let's look at them in detail.

Lead generation

Most companies have implemented a social media strategy to increase lead generation. As millions of users are connecting every day with different social media sites, every business is trying to have some customers somewhere on these sites. Companies can easily track the person by analyzing who likes the Facebook page of the company. Consequently, by getting more and more followers on the page, companies can increase their chances of generating new customers. The main difficulty is to inspire people to visit the particular page on social media sites. To make visitors stay around, the company's social media sites must present the company efficiently and make some associations with the users by sharing useful content, offering helpful information, and responding to all queries asked. Once the visitors showed some interest in the brand; then only, they will become valuable leads.

Brand exposure and awareness

The main benefit obtained by businesses is implementing social media policies that represent the increase in brand exposure. Brand exposure occurs when the client becomes aware of a product or service. For current brands, social media platforms also raise awareness among customers. Exposure is the primary step for new brands. The marketer can use social media channels for promotion of their products and services. The brand's social media pages can help companies to present the products and services interactively. Consumers can easily read reviews and comments about these products. Marketing through social media increases brand recognition by extending the online presence of the products and brands. When a business widely used social media platforms, it becomes essential to measure the impact of Social Media Marketing on brand awareness. Metrics can be measured with social media metrics. The social media metrics are social media exposure, influence, and engagement, which are as follows:

- **Social media exposure:** Social media exposure metrics shows the total number of people who can approach with a message or show interest in a brand through social media. It includes the number of visits, views, followers, fans, and subscribers.

- **Engagement:** Engagement metrics represent the number of people reading messages and showing interest in them. It includes the number of clicks, re-tweets, replies, shares, wall posts, and comments. Various tools can be used to measure the engagement. Brand exposure is the initial stage of the customer relationship. Social Media Marketing is an excellent way to take this step. By reading a post on social media pages, the consumer knows that the brand is active online and provides information to them to take a step towards the brand, product, or service. Further, awareness leads to consideration and purchase. Consequently, customers can become the regular purchaser.

- **Influence:** The influence metrics are more subjective and depend on the company's viewpoint of positive, neutral, or negative impacts. They represent the share of sentiment, voice, and the top influencers report.

Targeted traffic

Social media sites make a base for people who are trying to market products and services to people. Social media marketing is a beneficial way to push targeted traffic to companies' website. Social media sites will push targeted visitors back to the company's website. Companies can easily find the back link and interested referrals by creating more channels. To specify targeted traffic, we should define traffic first. Traffic happens whenever a person visits a particular website. There are a lot of techniques to get traffic to websites. With the increase in traffic, companies can reach thousands of visitors every day. Targeted traffic is specific traffic that reaches a website. It is when the audience reads an advertisement for a product or service that a brand is advertising on its website and they are engaged in purchasing that product, and for that, they click the link to go to the company's website. One of the most significant advantages that promotion through social media can allow marketers to target customers based on different factors. Social media sites are storing various kinds of data of their users, such as name, age, gender, geographical location, interests, and other information. Also, this data can be helpful to reach the company's target audience. Consequently, marketers can deliver messages related to marketing directly to those people who are most likely to see them and click on them.

Furthermore, search engines also love social media. Most search engines are paying significant amounts to social media channels as they are interactive and always provide real-time data. When one social media page gets the number one place on Google, it will heighten the traffic to the company's website. All the traffic generated from social media channels can improve the consumer's judgment of the brand.

People trust company mostly when they are referred by people they know. Social media is entirely about building healthy relationships. Businesses can get traffic directly from the content they publish on social media pages and also from the people who read the material, like it, share it, or talked about it.

Market insights – research and competitor monitoring

Social media has transformed the way of market research and competitor monitoring. Social media channels offer the opportunity to view competition. Competitive benchmarking is an essential part of any social media policy. Each brand has its plans, goals, and execution tactics. Nevertheless, brands and their competitors are usually trying to reach and engage with the same consumer database. Several tools exist that help marketers to analyze about the strategy of their competitors. First, it helps to examine the competitor activeness on their social media sites every day, the number of websites they have created and updating, the frequency of posting, and more importantly, analyze the reaction of the people to their posts. The use of social media to research competitors gives worthy information for any business that is looking to implement a smart social media marketing strategy. Following the competitors' activities offer insights into plans that are successful and that are not, thus helps in decision making. Additionally, finding out the reaction of consumers about the brand, product, and services by comparing to its competitors that are offering related products and services. It helps the business to strengthen the points that customers like, and make modifications where they feel that the company is lacking. On the other hand, the data available on the social media channels also directly affect the target audience. Indeed, by analyzing the data of the people interaction provide marketers with demographics and behavioral characteristics of their people. It helps to understand the target audience, its needs, and expectations. This information leads the social media marketing strategy of the company and helps to improve it. Marketers will apply the best marketing techniques and create enough marketing message to influence their target market directly. Subsequently, social media channels offer the opportunity to examine the marketing campaigns and aggregate feedback before investing the money in the target market. It will help the company to get a better understanding of the way to reach the target audience more effectively.

Customer interaction – customer service and feedback

Social media channels represent an extensive interactive dialogue between brands and their prospective customers. Through the social media sites, consumers can share their opinions and leave feedback easily along with asking for help and support. Marketers can have straight conversations with the people who are buying their products or services, or who are currently examining for products they have to offer. On the company pages, blogs, and profiles, customers can give feedback, by expressing their real thoughts and feelings regarding a company and its products and services. Marketers get the chance to answer these thoughts, along with providing information to educate the customers. These ideas help brands improve their consumers' experience. Feedbacks include general impressions of the brand, satisfaction with the buying process, and the way that customers feel about the appearance and usability of the company's website. Consumers can leave negative opinions also. If a negative opinion goes viral through social media's global interconnected platforms, marketers should have the efficiency to provide a quick and efficient response. The main aim is to monitor, identify, and solve problems immediately before they turn out of control. Company's strategies to offer such a quick, dynamic, and personalized customer service, consumers will acknowledge it and feel different. Encouraging the customer service is also a way of exhibiting the brand, products, and services interactively. This customer interaction on social media platforms is also reducing costs, as the community also helps to answer the problems. The cost per interaction in customer support is also cheaper through the social media sites than using the telephone or email support.

Cost-effective marketing techniques

Social media marketing does not need high advertising costs or a much higher amount of time. It follows a strategy of doing best and cost less business marketing.

Public relations and human resources

Another significant benefit for businesses implementing a social media approach is regarding the areas of public relations and human resources. Public relations professionals use it every single day to get feedback from clients, to interact with customers and to give responses to questions or problems. Social media like LinkedIn supports the hiring system in many ways. It helps in exploring new candidates, keeping in meeting with them, showing specific jobs, promoting to build company profile, making an employer brand. Public relations and social media both are creating and promoting relationships. Professional networking has been made exponentially easier with social media. Nowadays, networking signifies the ability to tap into several relevant connections with the single click of a button. Let's see the functional area benefits of public relations and human resources:

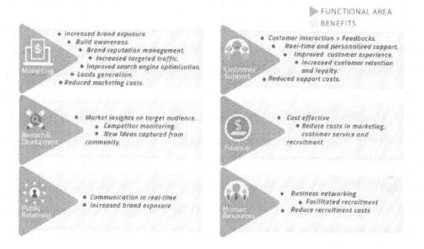

Figure 7.2: Functional areas and benefits of public relations and human resources

The current progress of FAIR for advancing socialmedia

This topic emphasizes the effort of the company in focusing on the research and development by establishing **Facebook Artificial Intelligence Research (FAIR)** that is responsible in making the networks of users more efficient to be used and utilized.

Facebook manages its business by getting knowledge about its clients and retrieving their information for advertisers. It then reinvests this money into offering new, useful functionality, for example, it is investing in videos and shopping, which can be used to personalized knowledge about a customer. As millions of individuals were uploading photographs and updating their status at every moment, up to this point Facebook would like to get an incentive from this unstructured information.

Deep learning techniques enable machines to figure out how to classify information independent of anyone else. A straightforward representation is a deep learning image analysis tool which would figure out how to observe pictures that contain cats, without being told what a cat resembles. This is the fundamental principle behind the primary use of DL in Facebook, and as DL algorithms turn out to be more advanced, they can be easily connected to more information that users share such as content, pictures, and videos. Let's see the areas in which FAIR is employing its current research:

Figure 7.3: Different areas and in which FAIR is employing its current research

Here are some use cases where DL is used to help Facebook achieve its goals in knowing more about its users:

- **Textual analysis:** The text is a popular form of communication on Facebook. A large proportion of the data shared on Facebook is still text. Video may involve larger data volumes. A picture may paint 1,000 words, but if someone wants to answer a simple question, then there is no need of 1,000 words. Every bit of data that is irrelevant to solve, the problem is just a noisy data, and a waste of resources to store and analyze. Following the various ways of content, writing is used on Facebook that can help to improve people's experiences with the different products. Understanding the various ways of content writing is used on Facebook that can help to improve people's experiences with the different products. With this goal in mind, Facebook uses the concept to build **DeepText**. It is a deep learning-based text understanding engine. It can understand the textual content, learn and analyze several thousand posts per second, spanning more than 20 languages with near-human accuracy. DeepText leverages deep neural network architectures that include convolutional and recurrent neural nets. It can perform learning based on word-level and character-level. Neural networks examine the association between words to understand how their meaning changes, depending on the other words around them. To train a model, they used **FbLearner Flow** and **Torch**. Trained models are served with a click of a button through the FBLearner predictor platform that provides a scalable and reliable infrastructure for model distribution. Facebook engineers can quickly build new DeepText models through the self-serve architecture that DeepText delivers.

- **Facial recognition:** Facebook AI research team builds **DeepFace**. It is a facial recognition system that is capable of matching faces in images with nearly the same accuracy as humans. It identifies human faces in digital images. It is trained with four million photos from Facebook. It is able to recognize the image of a person with an accuracy of around 97 percent. The DeepFace system uses a 3D modeling technique that can detect faces, crop, and warp them. It can scan millions of photos, virtually rotate and correct the images, and find all matching fronts. The DeepFace algorithm works by following four significant steps that include detecting, align, represent, and classify:

  1. **Face detection:** Face detection identifies human faces in digital image. The detected face is cropped and used as input for the next, that is, the alignment step. For face detection, the DeepFace algorithm used already developed Face Detection algorithm.

  2. **Face alignment:**
     - **2D alignment:** First, detect six fiducial points to scale, rotate, and translate the picture. The fiducial points are identified using Support Vector Regressor.

     - **3D alignment:** First, detection of 67 fiducial points using Support Vector Regressor is completed, then we compare them with a fixed 3D model of a general face. Re-construct the 3D model of the detected face and generate the 3D-aligned version of the crop. The final image is given to the deep neural networks.

  3. **Representation:** Three types of networks are used for representation, that is, convolutional networks, locally connected networks and fully connected networks.
     - Convolutional networks extract low-level features.

- Locally connected networks extract high-level features.
- Fully connected networks capture correlation between features located in scattered parts of the face image.

4. **Classification:** Images are recognized and classified by identification.
   - **Targeted advertising:** Facebook uses deep neural networks to decide which advertisements to show to which users. This is done by machines themselves to find out and cluster users together in the most insightful ways to give advertisements.
   - **Designing AI applications:** Facebook decides that the task of determining the processes that can be improved by AI, and machines can handle DL. The system called Flow has been implemented, which uses the concept of DL analysis to run simulations of around 300,000 ML models every month that allows engineers to test ideas and pinpoint opportunities for efficiency.

Application of AI in the field at Facebook scale

Social media stimulates innovation, drives cost additions, and empowers brands through mass collaboration. Contrariwise every industry, companies are using social media platforms for marketing and hype up their services and products, along with observing the views of the audience about their brand. The merging of social media and big data gives birth to a new level of technology. Every day, users feed Facebook with a lot of data. At every 60 seconds, upload around 136,000 photos, post around 510,000 comments and update 293,000 statuses. That is a LOT of data.

At first sight, this data may not seem useful. But with the detailed analysis of this type of data, Facebook can be able to recognize who our friends are, where we are, what we look like, what we are doing, about likes, dislikes, and much more.

Facebook is the company that maintains this high level of detailed customer information. Apart from analyzing user data, Facebook has other ways of determining user behavior, which are as follows:

- **Tracking cookies:** Facebook track users beyond the Web by monitoring cookies. If a user is logging into Facebook and concurrently browses other websites, Facebook can follow the sites they are visiting.

- **Tag suggestions:** Facebook suggests the user to tag a person in photos by image processing and facial recognition.

- **Facial recognition:** Facial recognition and image processing capabilities are the latest investments of Facebook. Facebook can easily track its users beyond the internet and other Facebook profiles with image data provided by user sharing.

- **Analyzing the likes:** Facebook can predict data accurately on a range of highly sensitive personal attributes by examining a Facebook Likes by users. The patterns of Facebook likes can accurately predict the sexual orientation, intelligence, religion, emotional stability, alcohol use and drug use, relationship status, race, age, gender, and political views, satisfaction with life.

Social media analytics

Social media analytics is the science of extracting valuable hidden business insights from social media data. Social media analytics are of various types among like descriptive analytics, diagnostic analytics, predictive and forecast analytics. Let's see them one by one:

- **Descriptive analytics:** Descriptive social media analytics answers the question of what happened and what is happening? Descriptive analytics aggregate and describe social media data in the form of reports, visualizations, and make clusters to understand well-defined business problems. Social media user comments are analyzed that comes under the descriptive analytics category. Comment analysis can be used to understand the sentiments of users' or identification of emerging trends by clustering topics.

- **Diagnostic analytics:** Diagnostic social media analytics finds the answer of why something happened? For example, diagnostic analytics can extract the data into a single view to see what worked in past campaigns and what didn't.

- **Predictive and forecast analytics:** Predictive analytics involves analysis of massive amounts of aggregated social media data to predict a future event. Thus, it deals with the question of what will happen and why will it happen? For example, an intention expressed over social media such as a buy, sell, recommend, desire, or wish can be mined to predict a future event. Forecast analytics is also known as **prescriptive analytics**. Prescriptive analytics suggest the best action to take while handling a scenario. In another word, we can say that by using optimization and simulation algorithms to advice on possible outcomes and answer: *What should we do?*

The following diagram illustrates the use cases of social media analytics divided into different domains:

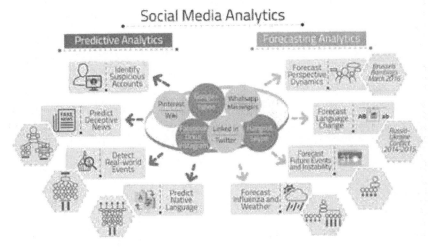

Figure 7.4: Use cases of social media analytics divided into different domains.

Let's discuss them in detail:

- **Identification of Fraud detection:** Fraud prevention is becoming a significant driver for the financial services industry. Fraud damages financial performance at a time when companies are being forced to reduce their cost-to-income proportions. Damage in reputation is hard to improve which leads rapidly to considerable loss of customers and market share. Financial services organizations face various challenges such as different transaction systems, gradually fraud detection solutions, and high operational costs with added security. Powerful fraud detection and management system are essential to handle finances. Failure in this area brings risk in banking and reputation. The right fraud solution could deliver enormous benefits across the business which includes driving down risks and cost, improving customer delight, and enabling modification. Active fraud detection can transform business accomplishment for financial services organizations in many ways like:

o   Higher visibility of exposure across channels.

o   Faster and more efficient fraud detection.

o   Protection for companies brand and reputation.

o   Improved retention of customers.

o   Reduced financial loss due to fraud which leads directly to the improvement in economic performance and higher value for sharers.

- **Predict deceptive news:** Fake news detection is defined as the prediction of the chances of a particular news article such as the news report, editorial, and expose being intentionally deceptive. False information can be created and advertised quickly through the web and social media platforms, which results in the broad real-world impact. False information can be categorized based on its intent and knowledge content, as described in the following diagram:

Figure 7.5: Hierarchy of False Information

- **Categorization based on intent:** False information can be classified by the intent of the reporter, as misinformation and disinformation. Misinformation is published without the intent to deceive. Therefore, common causes of misinformation include distortion of an original piece of accurate information, due to lack of understanding or attention. The writers then spread misinformation unconsciously to others through comments, blogs, articles, tweets, and so on. Disinformation is broadcasted with the intent to deceive. Deception on the Web occurs for many purposes. The audience leads most web disinformation campaigns to concentrate on influencing public opinion or directing online traffic to websites to earn money through advertisements.

- **Detect real-world events:** On social media sites, vast amounts of user-generated content are created every day. Real-World event detection has become a vital trend in the field of user-generated content analysis, the difficulty being to summarize and categorize uncoordinated communications from various users. Message posting to friends or forwarding received ones, connecting to new friends, and provide near real-time prediction of new events. Political events, accidents, festivals, and natural disasters represent that real-world events were happening at a particular location and time. Hence, event discovery and analysis from social media can be of vital importance, for example, for emergency response. In an earlier time, most works in the field of event detection focused on the analysis of text as well as meta-tags such as geolocation, timestamps, and so on. But now, it is possible to analyze real-world events in a given geographic region by using various deep learning algorithms.

- **Predict native language:** Based on user-generated content from a social media platform, it is also possible to fetch user profiles and predicts their gender, age, and geographic location.

Potential use of DL in improving customers among social media users

Social media analytics has grown from just being a tool for collecting users' likes and comments to an opportunity to achieve critical business insights to make quick and active decisions. By expanding social media analytics with predictive abilities, organizations can more accurately forecast the likes and dislikes of the customers and their actions. Predictive analytics includes the use of regression models and superior techniques, such as neural networks, to provide a 360-degree view of customers and their future activities based on their social-media and other data.

The following are areas where social media analytics can have a significant impact:

- **Innovation:** Product development teams can hit with social media to understand the likes or dislikes of the customers about a brand; the product features that a target demographic wants, along with the popular features of competitors' products. This information can be used to correct errors in the next iteration, find new ideas, and also reconsider current ideas and products in development. Most campaigns now use social media to feed ideas and contributions. Feedback on further product demonstrations can also provide inputs on client preferences in various markets.

- **Sales:** Predictive analytics, such as stock or market-basket analytics provides details about the products that are usually brought together, as well as the right combination of goods and services for customers – such as the combination of game and a movie based on the play. This information can be used for selling, and customizing products and services. Customer sentiment can be used to forecast sales and revenues, and prepare in advance for the problem in advance.

- **Marketing:** Nowadays, companies cannot rely upon analyzing old customer chatter to devise today's marketing campaigns. Social media analytics helps businesses to cope with rapid-changing customer choices through real-time marketing. By discovering trending, companies can quickly set tweets and social media updates to regulate with items, stay relevant, and manage customer engagement. Many companies use social media analytics to monitor the customers in real-time and adjust ad campaigns according to the requirement of the media users. Companies can also use image recognition technologies to see the images that are being shared by customers and find their impact on sales.

- **Competitive intelligence:** In business, nothing is more important than stable competitive information. Social media analytics allow companies to track multiple competitors on social media, and understand how competitors are using various social media platforms for promoting brand and customer engagement. Monitoring reviews and posts by bloggers about competitive products can provide worthy information that can be used to improve various functions across the business.

- **Customer service:** Social media channels can also help companies to identify customer service matters before they damage the reputation of a brand. By continuously monitoring real-time feedback from social media channels during a product release, the team of customer service can recognize issues and reach out to customers to fix glitches. Customer service can also forecast the type of problems customers may face during specific times and prepare accordingly.

Deep learning is a method in computer science where algorithms are intended and trained to be efficient and accurate as capable of making different predictions on data, such as classification and visual recognition. The significant advantage is that the networks train themselves by training on the same data to learn the structures and contexts of the data. The data is mostly in the form of electronic data and further use for analysis. The data are of different types such as numbers, names, and categories from different communications with the environment and human beings. The vital aspects of the data are the size and quality of the information. The data of better quality is used in training, the better success, and result of predicting data in the future.

The algorithms can be trained with different learning techniques where supervised learning and unsupervised learning are two conventional techniques. The primary difference between these techniques is that in supervised learning, data is labeled and known for the trainer which makes this technique suited for classification and regression problems. While in unsupervised learning, the information is not labeled. So, it is efficient for clustering problem where algorithms can discover different types of patterns within the unlabeled data. DL exists in many areas such as object recognition, speech, and audio processing, and sentiment classification. A DL model is described as a model which consists of two neurons, input, and output, where data is forward through the input layer. The input layer transmits the data onto the hidden layers, where it is examined at different levels. Let's take an example of an image; each hidden layer will review the pictures on various levels, from pixel-level to the whole picture and then the output layer predicts the representation of an image. DL can be used in various learning scenarios such as supervised, unsupervised and hybrid networks and for various other problems such as classification, regression, and vision.

With the current advances in DL, the capacity of algorithms to analyze the text has enhanced considerably. Inventive use of advanced AI techniques can be a useful tool for doing in-depth analysis. It is essential to classify incoming buyer conversation about a particular brand based on the following points:

- Critical aspects of a brand's product and service that customers care.
- Intentions and reactions of users concerning the aspects.

The following are the basic concepts when used together become an essential tool for analyzing billions of brand talks with human-level accuracy:

- **Sentiment analysis:** Sentiment analysis is a method of data mining, where text can be analyzed to learn the sentiment of the text. More formally, the polarity of the emotions, opinions, sentiments, evaluations, appraisals, attitudes, and emotions behind the text, that is to determine whether it is positive, negative or neutral, happy or sad, and so on. Sentiment analysis can help to find the feelings of the people about a particular topic. For example, the data is collected from Facebook, where the user talks relating to the particular topic and the sentiment of the text are determined. With the volatile growth of social media (for example, forum discussions, blogs, reviews, micro-blogs, tweets, comments, and posts on social networking sites) on the web, individuals and businesses are frequently using the content of these media for decision making. The following figure shows different sentiments of different people:

Figure 7.6: Representation of the different sentiments in a crowd.

Nowadays, if someone wants to buy a product, it is no longer needed to get reviews from friends and family because there are many reviews by users and discussions in public forums about the product on the web. For businesses, there may no longer be necessary to conduct surveys, opinion polls, and focus groups to gather public opinions because such information is abundant publicly available. Sentiment analysis is useful in consumer market to get reviews related to products, marketing to know attitudes and trends of consumers, social media to find the opinion about recent hot events in town, movie to see whether a recently released movie is a hit.

The applications are classified into the following categories:

    o **Applications to review- websites:** Event review, movie reviews, product reviews, and so on.

    o **Uses as a subcomponent technology:** Detecting hostile, lousy language in emails, spam detection, context-sensitive information detection, and so on.

    o **Applications in business and government intelligence:** To know about consumer attitudes and trends.

    o **Applications across different domains:** To get information about public opinions for political leaders or about rules and regulations and so on.

- **Emoji analysis:** An emoticon is speed writing for facial expression. It allows the user to show their feelings, emotions, moods, and arguments with non-verbal words in a written message. It helps to draw the attention of readers along with enhancement and improvement in the understanding of the word. An emoji is developed with modern communication technologies that promote more meaningful messages. An emoji is a graphic symbol that represents facial expressions along with several other concepts and ideas, such as weather, celebration, vehicles, buildings, food, drink, animals, plants, or emotions, feelings, and activities. The following figure represents different emojis with their key emotions:

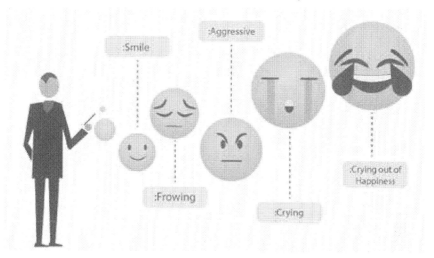

Figure 7.7: *Representation of different emoji with their key emotions.*

- Brands are always enthusiastic to see that they please their customers online may find some interest in the number of positive or negative emojis used in combination with their Facebook handles.

How is the 🍑 used on twitter ?

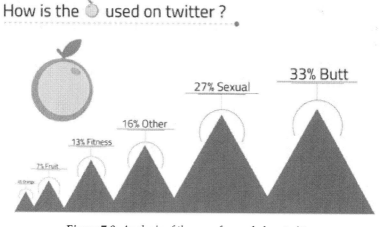

Figure 7.8: *Analysis of the use of a symbol on twitter*

- **Intent analysis:** Deep learning algorithms can analyze a string of text and indicate the intention underlying it. Sentiment analysis is an NLP technique which gives whether the nature of a particular text is positive, negative or neutral.

Though the intent analysis goes a level deeper and gives an idea of whether a string of text is a complaint, a suggestion or a query. Valuing the intent of messages on social media opens a lot of new possibilities.

Now, if someone runs sentiment analysis on tweets, it returns a positive or negative sentiment only but we run the intent analysis, it can analyze and judge whether the tweet is a suggestion or a query. Some of the most important use cases of intent analysis are discussed as follows:

o **Targeting ads:** Intent analysis can help in determining the placement of ads. Once we extract intention of text from the social media posts, it becomes simpler to recognize the pattern. Companies can target the ads to the audience by getting the information from the intent analysis results. For example, let someone post on social media about recent product experience, and it has many other comments tagged along with that post. It becomes easy to extract the intent from the text on the page. If the intended results are questioning about the services of the mentioned brand, companies can display advertisements and provide better offers.

o **Customer handling:** One of the most realistic applications of intent analysis is the management of customer services. If the intention of the existing customer in the posts is detected and managed, becomes a lot easier to resolve the issue. Companies can prioritize complaints from the customers and respond to them without wasting much time.

o **Complete social media analysis:** If companies track the competitors' brands on social media, use of the intent analysis is significant. The public posting platforms are an outstanding source of performing a substantial part of online marketing and making random posts to reduce time. So, tracking of the success or failure remains obscure even after running sentiment analysis. Once the jobs are segregated by the intent of the posts, marketers can do the review of the relevant ones. It helps the social media marketers to separate noise from the corpus and focus on the opinion and feedback related to the text.

o **Contextual Semantic Search (CSS):** CSS is an intelligent search algorithm that is specially designed for the classification of textual data based on the related concept. CSS takes thousands of messages as input and filters all the messages that closely match with the given concept. CSS is an advanced text classifier powered by DL. An intelligent AI technique is used to convert every single word into a specific point, and the distance between these points is used to classify messages, where the context is similar to the concept that users are exploring. The following graphic describes how CSS represents a significant improvement over existing methods used by the industry:

Figure 7.9: Graphic describes how CSS represents a significant improvement over existing methods used by theindustry

A conventional strategy for filtering all cost-related messages is to do a keyword search on cost and other closely associated words such as pricing, costing, charge, $, and paid. This method is not very practical as it is impossible to think of all the associated keywords and their variants that represent a distinct concept. On the other hand, CSS takes the name of the idea (which is *cost* here) as input and filters all the words having similar context even if variants of the concept keyword are not mentioned.

Conclusion

Facebook, a leading social media giant is adopting AI with its both hands. According to Facebook, the prime use of AI for Facebook is for providing connections and for providing security. For handling this purpose separately, Facebook already established its AI research wing, which is known as FAIR. Under the umbrella of FAIR, Facebook is investing in most of the AI techniques such as DL and using these techniques for different applications such as Facial Recognition and much more. AI is the need of these social media companies because not only connections are essential, but to keep them secure is more important.

Questions

1. Describe some use cases of social media analysis.

2. Describe some advantages of Facebook.

3. What are the primary uses of deep learning in social media? Discuss each of them briefly.

4. Describe briefly about each step of the Facial Recognition procedure of Facebook.

CHAPTER 8

Personalized Intelligent Computing by Apple

Apple introduces innovative products and services every year. In this chapter, wepresent business strategies employed by the company, especially in adopting AI and DL. We'll discuss its business models and product development strategies with the latest technologies like DL. This chapter explores Apple's upcoming innovations based on the current trends of this highly secretive company.

Structure

- AI in Apple: from Siri to the image processing
- Innovation in intelligent product development
- Potential of DL in Apple's business model

Objective

This chapter will help you to understand DL's potential in innovative product development, anticipation of user expectations, and the need for intelligent products and services. This chapter briefly demonstrates the intelligent computing capabilities of Apple, as well as how deep learning can be used to enhance the skills of modern-day computing.

Introduction to Apple

Steve Jobs is the genius mind behind the famous and reputational Apple Company. Apple designs desktop computers, laptops, iTunes, iPods, iWatch, iOS, iPhones, andiPads. Apple has been in the business for some time and it has got great success; products designed by them are still growing in popularity. It is currently recognized as one of the best companies in the world of technology, revenue, and brand ranking.

Apple has worked hard for success. They took proper measures at all times and provide high quality and effective delivery of products and services. Apple follows various strategies. These strategies play a significant role in their success.

Apple's marketing strategy

Apple's marketing strategy is based on the philosophy that customers never know what they want. Subsequently, instead of conducting marketing analyzes to identify the needs and desires of the customer, the company prefers to introduce innovative features and abilities in their products. This strategy makes customers fond of Apple products.

Apple **segmentation, targeting, and positioning(STP)** represent the focus of its marketing efforts, as shown in the following diagram:

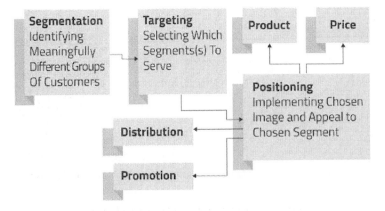

Figure 8.1: STP representation

Let's discuss them in detail:

- **Segmentation:** Segmentation involves separating the population into groups according to specific characteristics. There are several segmentation techniques used by Apple, and they are as follows:

  o **Demographic segmentation:** It is when the market is divided into segments of education, age, gender, income, occupation, and so on.

  o **Geographical segmentation:** It is when the market is divided into segments of location, city, region, state, country, and so on.

  o **Psychographic segmentation:** It is when the market is divided into segments of status, behavior, ethics, or values.

- **Targeting:** Targeting is choosing particular groups that are identified as a result of segmentation, to sell products. It is the second stage of the process. After the market has been separated into different segments, marketers select particular segments to target and put resources and efforts into that segment. There are different targeting methods that can be used by the company, that include the following:

  o One supplier targets a single segment with a single product. Refer to the following diagram:

Figure 8.2: Representation of One supplier with single segment with a single product system

o One supplier with one product targets all segments. Refer to the following diagram:

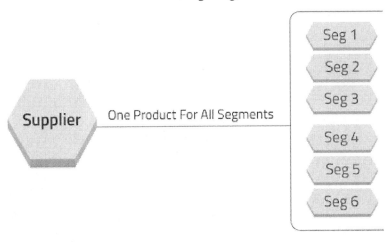

Figure 8.3: Representation of One supplier with one product for all segments system

o One supplier with several brands targets different segments for each brand:

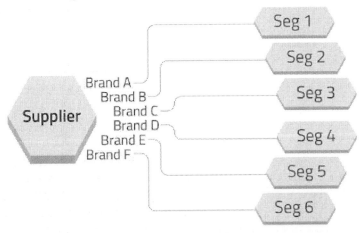

Figure 8.4: Representation of One supplier with different products for all segments system

- **Positioning:** Positioning is one of the most straightforward and useful tools for marketers. After segmenting a market and targeting a consumer, there is a need to locate a product within that market. Positioning is all about judgment, and it may vary from one person to another. Customers perceive Apple as a premium brand, and that is the reason it can demand a premium price. Therefore, Apple targets less price-conscious customers and differentiates itself from competitors by meeting the requirements of their targeted customers.

Siri technology

Siri is made of three technical components, which include a conversational interface, personal context awareness, and service delegation. Let's look at them in detail:

- **Conversational interface:** Siri's interface makes it possible to have a conversation with it. Whether it's task fulfillment or seeking a solution, Siri does it well. It is strengthened with language understanding components that are quite effective.

- **Personal context awareness:** Siri recognizes conversational intent that comprises location, time, task, and dialog contexts. Siri also knows about the friends of the user and additional information that is accessible to them.

- **Service delegation:** Siri is capable to merge vertical and horizontal searches across various information sources and edit them based on dynamic criteria that allow it to get tasks completed.

AI in Apple: From Siri to the image processing

Apple started the entire virtual assistant craze with Siri on the iPhone, many years ago. Siri is a personal assistant with a voice-controlled natural language interface. It was introduced in iOS 8 on iPhone 6. It uses sequential inference and contextual awareness to perform tasks for iOS users. On iPhone 6, the Hey Siri feature could only be used when the phone was charging. However, the ability of the iPhone was enhanced in subsequent generations, that is, 6S onwards and iPad. These generations used a low-power and always-on processor so that Siri could listen constantly. Thus, the *Hey Siri* feature became available for use at all times.

Siri is an AI program that consists of ML, NLP, and a web search algorithm. It empowers users of Apple iPhone 4S or later and latest iPad and iPod Touch devices to operate their mobile device and its applications by giving commands in simple language. Users can give commands (to send messages, calls, set reminders, manage iTunes) and receive confirmation audibly from Siri. To use Siri, there is no need to change the way one speaks; it is a natural language interface that understands regular speech. For example, when a user wants to create some reminder like *Remind me to go for a walk at 6:00 AM*, it responds with messages like *Ok, I added "go for a walk" to your reminders for tomorrow at 6 AM*.

Siri can work beyond multiple iPhone and iPad apps to achieve its tasks. It also supports extensive dictation that enables users to dictate to Siri. Users' speech is changed into text, and it is used in email, text messages, note-taking, web searching, Facebook status updates, and related operations.

- **Deep learning in Siri:** There are two types of speech synthesis techniques used in the business — unit selection and parametric synthesis. These techniques are explained below:
  o **Unit selection synthesis** produces high-quality speech recordings; therefore, it is the most extensively used speech synthesis technique in business products.
  o **Parametric synthesis** provides highly intelligible and fluent speech but suffers from lower quality. Therefore, parametric synthesis is used when a small footprint is required.

Modern selection systems merge some of the benefits of the two approaches and are known as hybrid systems. Hybrid unit selection uses the parametric approach to predict the units that are to be selected. DL has gained significant impulse in the field of speech technology, and parametric synthesis has benefited dramatically from deep learning technology. DL has additionally empowered a new approach for speech synthesis, known as direct waveform modeling, for example, using WaveNet, which can provide the flexibility of parametric integration and high quality of unit selection synthesis. However, given its extremely high computational cost, using it is not yet feasible on a production system.

Siri has powered the usage of a speech popularity unit present in smartphones, which runs within the heritage of the device all the time. This speech recognizer makes use of a **Deep Neural network (DNN)** that corresponds to the voice patterns that are, in addition, generated as a probability distribution for those voice sounds. A method known as Temporal Integration is used to compute a confidence score to check whether or not a command contains the phrase *good day Siri*. If the command is anywhere near the phrase Siri gets activated.

Apple uses DNN for face detection

Apple started using deep learning for face detection in iOS 10. With the arrival of deep learning and its various applications in computer vision problems, face detection accuracy increased significantly. Compared to conventional computer vision, the models in DL require more memory, more disk storage, and numerous computational resources.

The typical high-end devices were not suitable for the implementation of deep-learning vision models. Thus, cloud-based solutions came to the rescue. Images are sent to a server for analysis and detection of faces using DL inference. Apple's iCloud Photo Library provides a cloud-based solution to store photos and videos. Before sending any pictures and videos to the cloud storage, they are encrypted on the device and can be decrypted by methods that are registered with the iCloud account.

How face ID detection system works

As camera consists of various features like infrared camera, ambient light sensor, proximity sensor, flood illuminator, Dot projector, and more.

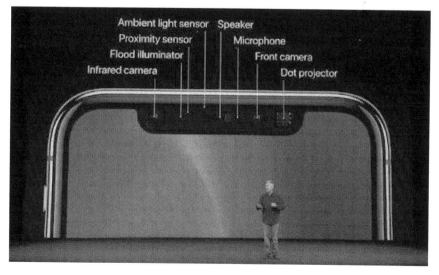

Figure 8.5: Showing different sensors used for face detection

True depth camera system

Every time a user looks at iPhone X, whether to unlock a screen or to authenticate to see an incoming notification, the right depth camera system detects the face with the flood illuminator even in dark conditions. When the face of the user is identified, Face ID authenticates and unlocks the device by checking that eyes are open and focused on the device.

Once it confirms the presence of an authorized face, the dot projector projects and reads over 30,000 infrared dots to form a map of the face, along with an infrared image. This data is further used to generate a sequence of 2D models and depth maps, which are electronically signed and forwarded to the Secure Enclave. The actual depth camera randomizes the series of 2D images and a depth map, and projects a device-specific random pattern.

Thus, the system uses the infrared image and the infrared dots, which are then pushed into neural networks to create a mathematical model of the users' faces.

Neural networks

Facial matching is performed using trained neural networks in real-time. Apple took a billion images, including IR and depth images. With that, it developed multiple facial matching neural networks and created Face ID technology with high accuracy for a diverse range of users. Face ID is built to work even if the subject is wearing hats, glasses, scarves, contact lenses, or sunglasses. Moreover, it is also designed to work indoors, outdoors, and in the dark. An added neural network is used in it that's trained to recognize and resist spoofing guards used to unlock the phone with photos or masks.

It's analyzed by the *Apple A11 Bionic chipset* and matched against data in the Secure Enclave on the iPhone.

Anti-spoofing mechanism in Face ID recognition

A spoofing attack is an attempt to access a device by using a photo, video, or any other proxy of an authorized person's face. Some significant examples of such attacks are as follows:

- **Video attack:** This is a more complicated way to trick the system, which usually requires a video of the victim's face. This approach replicates the facial movements of the victim to look more natural as compared to holding someone's photo in front of the device.

- **Print attack:** Attackers uses someone's photo. The image can be printed or displayed on a digital device.

- **3D mask attack:** During this type of attack, a mask is used as the medium for spoofing. It's an even more complex attack compared to attacks using video. Besides natural facial movements, it facilitates ways to beat some extra layers of protection like depth sensors.

In the latest hardware repetition, Apple has added excellent depth-mapping and 3D-sensing techniques that enable spoofing detection with high accuracy.

Other benefits of AI on smartphones

The following are the other benefits of AI on smartphones:

- **Camera benefits:** This is one of the critical areas on which iPhone makers are working. Using AI, the phone's camera interface can detect objects, such as a broom, landscape, food, fireworks, and so on, in the camera frame and adjust the settings accordingly to get the best possible image. AI can also identify facial features and enhance then automatically for an excellent portrait.

- **Language translator:** There are various translation apps available that allow users to take an image and get the text in it translated from one language to another. This is done with internet access; however, with AI, iPhone will be proficient at translating words in real-time without an internet connection.

- **User behavior:** An AI system is intended to learn and adapt as it is used over a period of time. On smart-phones, the AI can determine the usage pattern of users and learn from it on a day to day basis. When a user switches to silent mode after reaching work, turns on Bluetooth after reaching home, and closes the background-running applications after some time, AI recognizes these patterns and automates these daily tasks over time.

- **Improved security:** Apple iPhone X uses an AI-based algorithm as a Face ID to unlock the system. AI system works to recognize the user's face for protection. Using AI processing, iPhone X can locate look with changes like spectacles or beard over time.

- **Voice assistants:** Voice personal assistants have been around for some time now. Siri, Cortana, Google Assistant, and Alexa are various voice assistants that use AI to recognize speech and respond accordingly. Now, voice assistants have improved with improved AI integration. Instead of only replying to simple queries, they also perform other tasks, such as placing an online order, typing and sending a message, searching for particular songs, and more.

Innovation on intelligent product development

Apple is one of the companies that thrive in the market through its designs andinnovative products. For several years, Apple products have attracted users by winning the empathic design challenge. Regularly, each year, Apple introduces new innovative products on the market that are usually better compared to other computer and mobile companies in the market.

Apple has released the best-selling products and transformed entire industries on its own. With its growth in size and influence, phones, music, computers, and even advertising industries have been significantly affected. The following figure contains a list of current apple products.

Figure 8.6: Current Apple products

Emergence of Apple products year by year

- **In 1998 iMac debuted:** The first iMac was introduced in May 1998 with codename Columbus. It consisted of 256 MB RAM and a hard drive of 4 GB. It had macOS, which was introduced in 1997. This version of the iMac consisted of a 4 Mbps IrDA port and 56Kpbs modem. It also had two 12 Mbps Universal Serial Ports (USB) as it's only means of external expansion, and it also included a newly-designed USB keyboard and mouse.

- **In 2001, the iPod was introduced:** The iPod was launched in October 2001 with codename Dulcimer. With this, Apple marked its appearance in the digital music market. It could give competition with both hard-disk based and flash-based players. It consisted of 32 MB of RAM

- **In 2001, iTunes Store was introduced:** It was just less than a year ahead of iPod. iPod was a hardware medium for the iTune, which turned the fortune of Apple around.

- **In 2007, iPhone was released:** It was announced in January 2007 and released in June in the same year; with iPhone, Apple marked its entry into the phone market. Steve Jobs defined it as a wide-screen iPod with hand controls and said that it is a revolutionary mobile phone and a breakthrough internet communications device. The iPhone was considered the first Apple-branded consumer device to run on OS X.

- **In 2008, the MacBook Air was released:** It was announced in October 2008, and it was released late 2008. The MacBook (Aluminum, 13-inch) was powered by several features of the higher-end MacBook Pro (15-inch, Late 2008). In addition to the stunning new aluminum Unibody enclosure, the MacBook (13-inch, Aluminum, Late 2008) included a faster bus, faster graphics chipset, and a clickable Touch trackpad, which supported two, three, and four-finger gestures.

- **In 2010 the iPad was introduced:** Apple introduced the iPad as the first device in a thoroughly new market segment, with the claim that it will be better for many processes compared to traditional laptops or smartphones. The iPad imported specially redesigned adaptations of the standard suite of iPhone applications and redeveloped them from scratch to take advantage of the increased processing power and screen real estate.

Every company has its weaknesses and strengths. Apple also has a corner of weaknesses and strengths. Let us what are its strengths and weaknesses through the following figure:

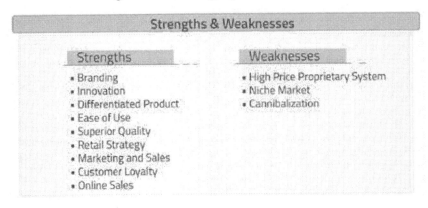

Figure 8.7: Some strengths and weakness of Apple

Conclusion

It is true that from a business point of view, Apple constructed a closed environment from its products and technologies. Still, so far, they were very successful in providing quality and quantity to customers. The products of Apple are considered expensive, and this acts as a drawback as these products are unaffordable for a sizeable chunk of users. However, owning Apple products is a status symbol for its buyer; this acts as a passive advantage for Apple products.

Apple does not compromise on the quality of products even if it means producing expensive products. Therefore, they have adapted to AI much earlier than some of the recognized IT giants. Currently, they are moving towards trying something different with AI, which is consistent with their tagline — Think Different.

Questions

1. Discuss the marketing strategy of Apple briefly.
2. Discuss the applications of DL in Apple.
3. Discuss the strengths and weaknesses of Apple products.
4. Discuss the use of DL in Siri.

CHAPTER 9

Cloud Computing Intelligence by Microsoft

Introduction

Microsoft has shown interest in joining the race of AI by redefining the roles of its research department, Microsoft Research. In this chapter, the efforts of the company in contributing to the development of AI and DL research are presented. The company's progress in AI can be seen in its cloud service Azure. The purpose of this chapter is to elucidate the use of cloud technology by Microsoft. Also, we'll discuss how Microsoft is enabling deep learning-based product development and strategizing business models with the cloud-based artificial intelligence services.

Structure

- Microsoft, DL, and cloud technology
- Preparing DL for business analytics
- Designing the business model and product development based on Microsoft services

Objective

By the end of this chapter, you will learn how Microsoft uses cloud technology to enable DL-based product development and strategizes business models with cloud-based AI services.

Microsoft Research AI is an organization that brings together the expertise across Microsoft Research to pursue game-changing advancements in AI. The research and development enterprise combines advances in ML and DL with innovations in language and dialogs, human-computer interaction, and computer vision to solve some of the most difficult challenges in AI.

They focus on examining the foundational principles of intelligence that include efforts to resolve the mysteries of human intelligence and use this knowledge to form a more general, flexible AI. Microsoft Research AI pursues the use of machine intelligence in different ways to enable people, organizations, and systems that deliver new expertise, with capacities that help them to be more efficient, occupied, and productive.

At Microsoft, researchers think of AI as a set of technologies that allow computers to understand, learn, design, and support in decision-making to resolve problems in ways similar to humans. With these abilities, computers are now more responsive compared to the past, when they could only follow pre-programmed instructions.

Long ago, Microsoft Researchers interacted with computers through a command-line interface. Moreover, while the graphical user interface was a significant step forward, they started interacting with computers just by talking to them. To enable these new capabilities, they teach computers to see, hear, understand, and reason.

- **Speech:** This is the capability of computers to listen to speech, make sense of it, and transcribe it into text.
- **Vision:** Vision is the ability of computers to recognize and comprehend the pictures or videos.
- **Knowledge:** This is the ability of a machine to reason by understanding relationships between people, places, things, and events. For instance, when you search for a movie on Google, it gives you additional information about the cast and other relevant films. Here, computer reasoning looks for additional information related to the original query.

- **Language:** This is the ability of computers to understand the meaning of words by taking into account noises and complexities of communication.

A lot of work still remains to be done to make these changes fully functional in everyday use. Computers still face some difficulties in understanding speech in a noisy environment where people talk over one another or with unfamiliar accents or languages. It is very challenging to teach computers to understand speech, analyze it, and make decisions based on them. To train computers to understand the meaning of more complex questions, they need to be trained to look at the big-picture, interpret and evaluate the context, and use background knowledge.

Microsoft Approach to AI

Immense amounts of data, fast processing power, and smarter algorithms are powering AI applications and associated use cases across consumer, manufacturing, finance, healthcare, transportation, and logistics sectors.

Moreover, government sectors around the world are enabling smarter and intelligent applications to speak, listen, and make decisions in unique ways. As AI technologies and deployments are applicable in virtually every industry, a wide range of use cases are there to illustrate the potential of business opportunities and inspire the need for change in existing business models.

Microsoft AI platform - Overview

The Microsoft AI platform extends a complete set of flexible AI services, enterprise-grade AI Infrastructure, and latest AI tools for data scientists and developers to create applications of the future. The AI platform consists of three major areas:

- **AI services:** Developers can quickly consume high-level finished services that stimulate the development of AI solutions. It comprises intelligent applications that are customized to the organization's availability, security, and compliance requirements.

- **AI infrastructure:** Services and tools are supported by infrastructure with enterprise-grade security, compliance, availability, and manageability.

- **AI tools:** This is about leveraging a set of large tools and frameworks to build, deploy, and operationalize AI products and services at scale. Also, it uses an extensive collection of supported devices and harnesses the intelligence with massive datasets through deep learning frameworks.

Technical Stack of Microsoft AI platform

Microsoft AI platform stack provides a rich set of interoperable services, APIs, libraries, frameworks, and tools that developers can use to build smart applications. The following figure provides an overview of the stack of Microsoft AI platform:

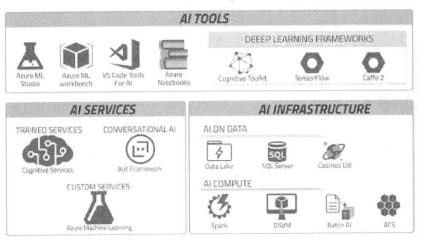

Figure 9.1: Microsoft AI platform stack

AI services

AI services consist of intelligent applications that are customized especially for an organization's availability, security, and compliance requirements with a broad set of flexible cloud AI services. Let's discuss the main components of the Microsoft AI platform one by one:

- **Cognitive services:** It uses AI to solve business problems. Businesses can introduce applications, websites, and bots with intelligent algorithms that can see, hear, understand and speak with ordinary methods of communication.

- **Azure machine learning:** It deals with the modeling of AI algorithms and experimentation with ease and it customizes solutions based on the requirements of the user.

- **Bot framework:** It stimulates development for conversational AI. It integrates with Cortana, Slack, Office 365, and Facebook Messenger.

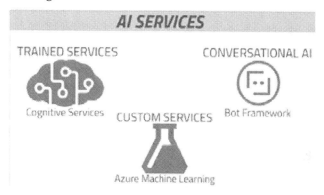

Figure 9.2: Different AI Services

Cognitive services

Microsoft cognitive services are a part of Microsoft's emerging portfolio of machine learning AP; they facilitate developers to merely add intelligent features within their applications. Cognitive services are a set of SDKs, APIs, and services available to developers to make their applications more intelligent and discoverable. Moreover, they help to develop apps with powerful algorithms to see, hear, understand, speak, and interpret commands using standard methods of communication.

With few lines of code, it supports customizable web services. Further, it adds intelligent features such as vision and speech recognition, emotion and sentiment detection, language understanding, and easy search across various devices such as Android and iOS. Cognitive services consist of the following services:

- **Speech:** It processes spoken language in applications.

- **Language:** It allows applications to process natural language, evaluate sentiments, and learn to recognize the requirements of the users.

- **Search:** It makes applications, web pages, and other experiences smarter with the Bing search APIs.

- **Knowledge:** It maps complex information and data to solve tasks such as semantic search and intelligent recommendations.
- **Vision:** Its various image processing algorithms help to build more personalized apps by delivering smart insights.

Azure machine learning

Azure machine learning is a predictive analytics and cloud-based service that helps to create and deploy predictive models quickly with analytics solutions. The ML service uses cloud-based technology that provides computer resource and memory flexibility. Moreover, it eliminates setup and installation concerns as it's accessible through web browsers on any internet-connected computer.

Azure machine learning service helps to build, deploy, and manage applications. It also helps to boost productivity and enables users to develop more straightforward tools and platforms.

Data Collection and Management   ML Studio   Web Services   Embedded ML Model

Figure 9.3: Steps in Azure machine learning services

Machine learning is a subcategory of artificial intelligence. Forecasting or prediction with the use of machine learning can make applications and devices smarter. For instance, it's easy to build recommendation systems in online shopping apps and websites, in which the system recommends additional products, which are relevant to a customer's original purchase, with the help of ML.

One can work by using ready-to-use libraries of algorithms and use them to create models and deploy predictive solutions quickly.

Bot framework

The bot framework helps to build bots that assist with different types of interactions with users. This framework designs the bot to have free flowing conversations. The communication is guided according to the choices or actions of users. The bot can use text strings or rich cards that contain text, images, and action buttons. Natural language interactions are possible, and this helps users to interact with bots in a logical and meaningful way.

A bot can be a simple system that matches queries with patterns and produces answers or it could be a sophisticated weaving of AI techniques with complicated conversational skills. The Microsoft Bot framework helps to create new experiences and reach the users at scale by quickly building and deploying solutions across channels that include Facebook Messenger, Cortana, Skype, Slack, and Bing. The following diagram illustrates the architecture of the bot framework:

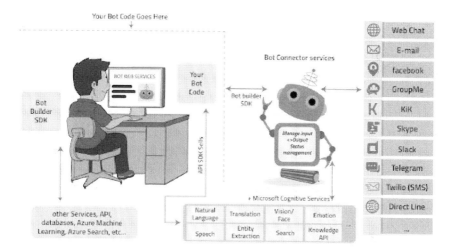

Figure 9.4: Complete architecture of Bot Framework

The bot framework is a platform used to build, connect, test, and deploy robust and intelligent bots. With the support for .NET, Node. js, and REST, users can get the Bot Builder SDK and instantly start building bots with the bot framework. Besides, users can also take advantage of Microsoft Cognitive Services to combine smart features like natural language understanding, image recognition, speech, and more.

The Azure Bot service provides a unified environment purpose to develop bots. The user can write a bot, connect, test, deploy, and manage through the web browser with no separate editor. For simple bots, there is no need to write code. It is powered by Microsoft Bot Framework and Azure Functions that makes the bot to run in a server-less environment on Azure.

AI infrastructure

Microsoft supports the power of virtually constant scale AI infrastructure along with integrated AI services. The following diagram shows the subcomponents of AI infrastructure:

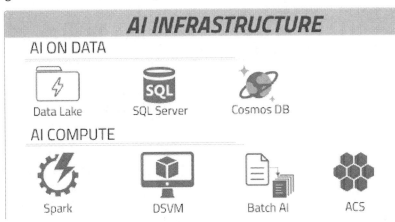

Figure 9.5: AI Infrastructure and its subcomponents

The subcomponents of AI are explained below:

- **AI compute:** It can compute services from a virtually infinite scale to the edge. The infrastructure provider will not only support AI functionalities but also integrate AI as a fundamental part of their infrastructure and service stacks.

  o **Batch AI training:** It experiences infinite elastic scale-out DL. It also performs massively parallel scale-out graphical processing unit (GPU) enabled AI development.

  o **Spark on HDInsight:** It leverages Apache Spark in the cloud for critical deployments.

  o **Data science VM:** It uses data science environment that contains modern tools for data exploration, development, and modeling activities.

  o **Azure container service:** It also deploys models of AI with the compliance of containers and scales them out automatically with Kubernetes. It turns AI models into web services using Docker containers along with auto-scaling and managing with Kubernetes.

- **AI on data:** Data alone doesn't help businesses to transform their organizations. Advanced analytics and machine learning contribute insights to data-driven choices that help to push the industry forward. Cognitive services inevitably democratize AI that makes every developer an AI developer. AI also enables the following data platforms:

    o **Data lake:** It helps to run transformations on data and AI on petabyte-scale.

    o **SQL Server 2017:** It uses various programming languages like R, Python, and native machine learning in an industry leading SQL database.

    o **Cosmos DB:** It integrates AI with distributed multi-model database storage.

- **AI tools:** The AI platform consists of the complete and productive toolkit for AI coding and management. It also enables developers to provide intelligence with extensive datasets through tools and in-depth learning frameworks. The following diagram shows the different AI tools under Azure:

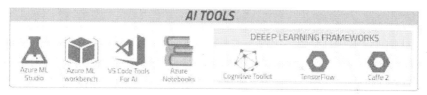

Figure 9.6: Different AI tools under Azure

Azure ML Studio

Azure ML Studio gives an interactive and visual workspace to build, test, and iterate on a predictive analysis model. One can easily drag-and-drop datasets and transform modules into an interactive canvas, connecting them to form an experiment that runs in machine learning studio. To iterate the design of the model, one can edit the experiment, save a copy, and rerun it. When required, the user can convert the training experiment to a predictive examination, and then publish it as a web service so that the model can be accessible to others as well.

Azure ML automatically sets up the model to work with Azure's load balancing technology. This technology helps the model grow and handle cloudburst scenarios, scaling-up, and shrinking down to meet user demands.

Azure ML Workbench

Workbench is an AI-powered data wrangling, experimentation, and lifecycle management tool. All processes together with Azure ML Workbench enable built-in data preparation that learns data preparation steps. Project management, running of history, and integration of notebook unleash the productivity. It leverages the open source frameworks such as Cognitive Toolkit, TensorFlow, Spark ML, and Scikit-learn.

Visual Studio (VS) Code Tools for AI

Visual Studio (VS) Code Tool makes building DL models easier, as there are in-built Azure machine learning services. Microsoft uses Visual Studio Code Tools for AI to create, debug, test, and deployment of AI on Windows and Mac for developers across desktop, cloud, and edge. With this tool, developers can develop deep learning models and call services straight from IDE.

Azure Notebooks

Azure Notebooks are helpful to organize datasets and Jupyter Notebooks at one centralizedlocation. For instance, Azure Notebooks can run **negative matrix factorization (NMF)** over large datasets efficiently and quickly identify topics of interest on feeds of Twitter.

Deep learning framework

AI platform stack maintains a vast array of deep learning frameworks that include MxNet, Cognitive Toolkit, Caffe2, TensorFlow, Chainer, Torch, Scikit-learn, and so on.

DL is affecting everything from healthcare, manufacturing to transportation. Businesses are using deep learning to solve difficult problems, such as image classification, machine translation, object recognition, and speech recognition.

Over the last five years, DNNs are AI models that have achieved widespread use. These neural networks surpass in feature creation automatically and process complex data types like text, images, audio, and videos. Common business use cases for DNNs are as follows:

- Determining whether uploaded audio, video, or text file contains some improper content

- Understanding a user's intent from their expressed or typed input
- Recognizing objects or people in a still image
- Translating speech or text from one language to another

Unfortunately, DNNs are considered among the most time and resource-intensive machine learning models. Applying a DNN to a single file may take thousands of milliseconds, and this processing rate is insufficient for some business needs. On the other hand, a trained linear regression model produces results in very less time. To handle the time issue, DNNs can be used in parallel – using a scalable fashion with Spark clusters. AI platform provides rich support for parallelism with Spark clusters.

Incorporation of DL capabilities in cloud computing

Microsoft includes DL capabilities in cloud computing. They provide a cloud machine learning (ML) platform and AI based cloud services like powerful text analysis, original language, computer vision, robust speech recognition, fast dynamic translation, smart search, and in-depth knowledge. AI is one of the powers of the new cloud computing generation. In this section, we will discuss AI capabilities in cloud computing, in the form of cloud ML platforms and AI cloud services:

- Google cloud machine learning platform is a fast, large-scale, and straightforward to use machine learning service. It provides advanced ML services, with pre-trained models and services to generate models.

- Google Cloud Vision API empowers developers to integrate vision detection features within applications easily. Features include image labeling, face detection, optical character recognition, and tagging of content.

- Amazon machine learning is a service that makes it easy for developers to use ML technology. Amazon machine learning provides visualization tools that help in the process of creating ML models without learning complex ML algorithms and technology.

- Microsoft Azure machine learning is a fully managed cloud service that lets developers build, deploy and share predictive analytics solutions. At Microsoft, the primary aim is to develop AI systems that will enable people to address local and global challenges.

Nowadays, AI enables faster and more significant progress in every field of human effort, and it is essential to allow the digital transformation. Every goal of a business or organization like engaging with customers, transforming products, optimizing operations, and empowering employees can benefit due to this digital transformation.

Providing adequate healthcare at a reasonable cost is one of society's most constraining challenges. AI can help in analyzing extensive amounts of patient data, identifying hidden patterns that can help toward better treatments, identifying new drugs or vaccines, and unfastening the potential of personalized medicine based on in-depth genetic analysis.

AI can transform how physicians diagnose diseases and improve health care. Machine reading can help physicians find relevant information in thousands of documents quickly. With this capability, it can help medical professionals spend more time on more significant work.

Providing safe and cost-effective transportation is another crucial challenge where AI can play an outstanding role. AI-controlled driverless vehicles can prevent accidents, improving traffic flow, and reducing carbon radiations, thereby saving thousands of lives and money every year. Here are examples of deep learning and AI:

- **Deep learning improves medical image analysis for clinicians:** AI systems help people to tackle significant problems. An excellent example is **InnerEye**, an AI based project developed by researchers at Microsoft that can treat cancer more effectively. InnerEye uses AI technology to analyze CT scans and MRI and helps physicians to treat cancer more quickly. Scans allow physicians to look deep inside a patient's body in 3D and study anomalies, such as tumors. For cancer patients who are undergoing radiation therapy, physicians use scans to tell tumors from the surrounding healthy tissues, bones, and organs. So, this technology helps to focus radiation on the tumor while avoiding the surrounding healthy parts as much as possible. To build Inner Eyes automatic segmentation, researchers used hundreds of CT and MRI scans. The reports were fed into an AI system and trained to recognize tumors. With further advances in the future, InnerEye may be helpful for mapping and tracking tumor that changes over time, and also able to assess whether a treatment is working.

- **AI helping researchers prevent disease outbreaks:** Another impressive example is Project Premonition. In recent years, we have seen the tragic stories of lives lost due to dangerous diseases like dengue that are transmitted from animals and insects to humans. At times, Epidemiologists are not even able to detect the emergence of these pathogens. Scientists and engineers at Microsoft researchers are exploring ways to detect pathogens in the environment, enabling health officials to prevent transmission even before an outbreak begins. Researchers use autonomous drones that are capable of operating through complicated environments to identify areas where mosquitoes breed. Further, they use robotic traps that differentiate between pathogen carrying mosquitoes and other insects, by analyzing wing-movement patterns. Once the samples are collected, advanced AI-based systems recognize the pathogens carried by mosquitoes. In the past, this kind of analysis took several months, but now with the AI capabilities of Project Premonition, this takes about 12 hours.

- **AI helps people with low vision:** Another domain where AI has the potential to have a substantial positive impact is in serving more than a billion people in the world with disabilities. A Microsoft platform called Seeing AI that is available in the iOS app store can support people struggling with blindness and low vision. The platform was developed by an engineer who lost his eyesight at seven years of age. This powerful app shows the potential of AI; it can help people with disabilities by capturing images from the user's surroundings and immediately describing the happenings around them. For instance, it can read menus and signs, identify products through barcodes, interpret handwriting, count currency, depict scenes, and identify objects. This application can be helpful during a meeting; it can tell the user that there is a man or a woman sitting across the table along with the sentiments of that person, that is, whether the person is smiling, sad, or paying close attention.

- **AI helps farmers to be more productive and increase their crop yield:** As the population of the world is expected to grow by nearly 2.5 billion over the next century, sufficient availability of food has become a matter of concern. AI offers essential opportunities to farmers that help them increase food production by improving agricultural yield and reducing waste. For instance, the **FarmBeats** project uses advanced AI technology and the power of the cloud to empower data-driven farming facilities at a low cost. This helps farmers with easily interpretable insights that help them improve crop yield by lowering overall costs and reducing the environmental impact of farming.

Microsoft business model

Microsoft generates revenue by developing, improving, licensing, and supporting a broad range of software products. They offer various services that include cloud-based services to businesses and consumers. They design and manufacture devices that integrate with its cloud-based services and deliver appropriate online advertising to a global audience.

Microsoft customers mostly include individual consumers, organizations, and application developers. Individual consumers make their own decisions to buy the devices they use. They obtain Microsoft products through distributors and resellers. Revenue is generated from individual consumers, office consumers, devices, gaming, and licensing of the Windows operating system.

Microsoft serves organizations of several sizes, including small and medium-sized organizations, large global enterprises, public sector enterprises, internet service providers, and various academic institutions. The company offers license programs, consulting services, enterprise-wide support, and several other specialized services to the organizations.

Microsoft generates revenues from organizations by voluminous licensing of the Windows operating system, dynamics business solutions, enterprise services, server products and services, and advertising. The company also makes revenues from application developers, developer tools, and by training and certifications on various Microsoft products. Creating an active developer community is an essential goal of the Microsoft business model. This helps them to build platform-based ecosystems that are beneficial for network effects among application developers and users. The network effects benefit from accelerating growth and creating a substantial competitive advantage.

The following diagram shows the elements of the Microsoft business model. It shows how the money flows in and out from the different customer segments:

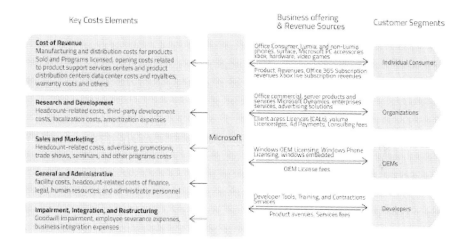

Figure 9.7: *Microsoft business model*

Microsoft's most significant expenses include employee remuneration, designing, building, retailing, and selling various products and services, data center costs in support of cloud-based services, and income taxes. The details of the critical cost elements are as follows:

- **Cost of revenue include the following:**
  - Manufacturing and distribution costs for goods sold and businesses licensed.
  - Operating expenses associated with product support service centers and distribution centers.
  - Costs incurred to incorporate software on PCs and drive traffic to its websites.
  - Expenditures incurred to give support and maintain internet-based products and services that include data center costs and royalties.
  - Inventory valuation adjustments.
  - Warranty costs.

o Expenses associated with the delivery of consulting services.

- **Research and development expenses include the following:**
    o Payroll, stock-based bonus expense, employee benefits, and other expenses associated with product development.
    o Localization costs incurred to translate software for international markets.
    o Third-party development and programming costs.
    o The reimbursement of purchased software code.

- **Sales and marketing (S&M) expenses include the following:**
    o Costs of advertisements, trade shows, promotions, seminars, and other relevant programs.
    o Payroll, stock-based bonus expense, employee benefits, and other expenses associated with sales and marketing personnel.

- **General and administrative expenses include the following:**
    o Legal, facilities, specific human resources, and other administrative personnel.
    o Individual taxes, legal, and other administrative fees.
    o Payroll, stock-based bonus expense, employee benefits, and other expenses associated with general and administrative personnel.

- **Impairment, restructuring and integration expenses include the following:**
    o Costs associated with the deterioration of goodwill and hypothetical assets linked to Microsoft's phone hardware business.
    o Systems incorporation and business integration expenses related to Microsoft's takeover of Nokia's devices and services business.
    o Employee division expenses.
    o Expenses associated with the incorporation of facilities and building operations related to restructuring exercises.

Microsoft business segments

Microsoft operated the business in five segments: Online Services Division, Windows Division, Microsoft Business Division, Server and Tools, and Entertainment and Devices division. These segments provide management with a complete financial view of the business.

The segments enable the arrangement of strategies and objectives beyond the regular division of development, sales, marketing, and services organizations. They also provide a framework for appropriate and balanced allocation of development, marketing, sales and services resources in businesses. These business segments are discussed in the following diagram:

Figure 9.8: Microsoft business segments

Let's discuss them one-by-one:

- **Online service:** The Online services division develops content and markets information to help people simplify tasks and make well-informed online decisions. It also allows advertisers to connect with audiences. Online services division offers include MSN, Bing, and Bing Ads. Microsoft also provides an independent algorithmic and funded search platform for websites worldwide. Bing and MSN make revenue through the sale of exploration and display advertising. Microsoft Bing is more than a standalone search engine now, and it has been integrated with new Microsoft products, such as Windows 8, the new Office, Xbox 360, and Windows Phone to intensify those offerings. They also plan to incorporate Bing into the product and service portfolio.

- **Window:** The Windows segment produces and markets **operating systems (OS)** for computing devices, associated software, online services, and PC accessories. This group of software, hardware, and services is intended to authorize individuals, businesses, and associations to explain everyday tasks in regards of the hardware and software. The revenue growth of the Windows segment was proportional to the growth of computing devices in the global market. Currently, around 65% of the total Windows segment revenue originates from Windows OS. Windows OS is purchased by original machine manufacturers who pre-install the OS on their devices. Apart from the market volume of computing devices, Windows revenue is influenced by the following:

  o The generation of different computing devices that emphasize mainly on the functionality of touch and mobility.

  o Attachment of Windows with the devices that are shipped.

  o Device market changes inspired by transformations between developed markets and developing markets along with consumer devices and business devices.

  o Variations in inventory levels within the original equipment manufacturers channel.

  o Changes in price and promotions that happen when the manufactured devices transfer from local system builders to large, multinational **original equipment manufacturers (OEMs).**

  o Sales of packaged software.

  o The demand of industrial customers for voluminous licensing and software support.

- **Server and tools:** This includes market software developer tools, server software, cloud-based services, and solutions that are designed primarily to make software developers, IT professionals, and their systems more productive and useful. Microsoft provides on premise software and cloud-based offers to bring together the advantages of traditional on-site offerings with cloud-based services. Server software is a combined server infrastructure and middleware that is designed to support software apps developed on the Windows Server operating system. This server software includes the server platform, business intelligence, database, storage, virtualization, management and operations, security, service-oriented architecture platform, and identity software. Server and Tools also make standalone and software development lifecycle tools for software architects, testers, developers, and project managers. Services can be run onsite at a partner-hosted environment or a Microsoft-hosted environment. Cloud-based services of Microsoft consist of a scalable OS with computing, database, storage, and management, along with complete cloud solutions, from which customers can build, deploy, and manage business workloads and web apps. These services also constitute a platform that helps developers create and connect applications and services on premise or in the cloud. The primary goal of Microsoft is to empower customers to give more resources for the development and usage of applications that profit their businesses, instead of managing on-premises hardware and software. Almost 80% of server and tool's income comes from product revenue, which includes purchases by licenses sold to OEMs, volume licensing programs, and retail packaged products.

- **Microsoft business:** Microsoft business segment contributions consist of the Microsoft Office systems like Office 365, SharePoint Office product set, Exchange, Lync, and Microsoft Dynamics business solutions, which may be delivered on premise or as a cloud-based service. Microsoft office is designed to increase organization productivity through a variety of programs, software solutions, services. It contributes over 90% of Microsoft business division's revenue. Growth of Microsoft Office depends on the capacity to add value to the Office product set and to continue to increase product enrichment in many other areas like enterprise search, content management, unified communications, collaboration, and business intelligence. Microsoft Dynamics products offer business solutions for supply chain management, financial management, customer relationship management, and analytics applications for start-ups, mid-size businesses, large organizations, and divisions of global companies. Around 85% of MBD revenue is produced from sales to businesses which include Office revenue created through volume licensing agreements subscriptions and Microsoft Dynamics revenue. Income from businesses commonly depends upon the number of licenses instead of the number of PCs sold in a given year. Almost 15% of MBD revenue is obtained from subscription sales, retail packaged products, and OEMs. This revenue is affected by the volume of PC purchases, the transformation in subscription-based licensing, and product launches.

- **Entertainment and devices:** The Entertainment and Devices division develops and exchanges products and services intended to cherish, entertain and connect people. The Xbox entertainment platform includes Kinect that is designed to give a unique range of entertainment options with the use of devices, content, peripherals, and online services. Skype is designed by Microsoft to connect family, friends, clients, and colleagues. The Windows Phone is designed to take users closer to the applications, people, and the content they need by providing unique abilities like Microsoft Office and Xbox LIVE. Through strategic collaboration, Windows Phone and Nokia are simultaneously creating innovative mobile products and services and spreading them to distinct markets. Entertainment and devices division revenue also include revenues from licensed mobile-related patents.

Conclusion

With Windows, Microsoft raised itself to the next level in the late 90s and early 2000s, but after the emergence of AI, the next challenge was to provide different products and services with empowered with AI. Microsoft is also catching up in the race of AI with products such as XBOX and services like Office 365. Also, they are using more AI in computational devices and software services offered to customers. It is pretty clear now that Microsoft is reviving itself using AI.

Questions

1. Discuss all the steps of Azure machine learning services.
2. Explain all Microsoft Business Segments in detail.
3. Discuss the Business Model of Microsoft.
4. Discuss the complete architecture of Bot Framework.